52 Wonders of Faith & Science for Horse-Loving Kids

Hoofprints of Hope

DEVOTIONAL

KATHRYN O'NEILL

Tyndale House Publishers
Carol Stream, Illinois

Visit Tyndale online at tyndale.com.

Visit Tyndale's website for kids at tyndale.com/kids.

Visit the author online at kathy-oneill.com.

Hoofprints of Hope Devotional: 52 Wonders of Faith and Science for Horse-Loving Kids

Designed by Eva M. Winters

Edited by Deborah King

Published in association with Steve Laube Agency, LLC

For manufacturing information regarding this product, please call 1-855-277-9400.

For information about special discounts for bulk purchases, please contact Tyndale House Publishers at csresponse@tyndale.com, or call 1-855-277-9400.

ISBN 979-8-4005-0163-0

Printed in China

32 31 30 29 28 27 26
7 6 5 4 3 2 1

For my husband, Wes, who has believed
in me and encouraged all my dreams.

TYNDALE KIDS

Faith & Science

BOOKS FROM TYNDALE KIDS

Ever wonder how faith and science work together?

Tyndale Kids Faith & Science books seek to foster a deep understanding of God's creation through the lens of science. The book must include one of the following:

1. the story of creation
2. experiments or lessons about a branch of science
3. elements of STEM or STEAM curriculum

Books in the Faith & Science Line:

Faith and Science with Dr. Fizzlebop: 52 Fizztastically fun experiments and devotions for families

Hoofprints of Hope Devotional: 52 Wonders of Faith and Science for Horse-Loving Kids

Quirky Critter Devotions: 52 Wild Wonders for Kids

The Size of Everything: Ginormous Galaxies, Itty-Bitty Quarks, and Me

The Super-Sized Book of Bible Activities Exploring Nature for Elementary

The Super-Sized Book of Bible Activities Exploring Nature for Preschool

Top 50 Bible Lessons with God's Amazing Animals

Top 50 Science-Based Bible Lessons: Exploring God's Truth through Science

Wake Up, Little Seed

Wonders of the Ocean Realm

Contents

Author's Note

I'VE ALWAYS LOVED HORSES. I was about ten when I decided a horse would fit in an abandoned shed in my yard. I clawed through clinging cobwebs to clean out that shed, sure I could convince my parents to get a horse. I couldn't, but I still dreamed of having a horse of my own someday.

I'd ride my green bicycle to the library every week. As the ocean breeze billowed the library curtains, I'd hunt for books about horses. *King of the Wind* by Marguerite Henry was my favorite, and I still have a copy. I'd pick out a Black Stallion book from Walter Farley's series and dream I was galloping the Black along the beach. His mane whipped around my face as we splashed through the shallows, sending seagulls screaming into the sky.

Though my dream of owning a horse has never

come true, the Lord has provided a special horse for me to ride wherever I've lived. Here are just a few I've loved: Webster, a big teddy bear of a Hanoverian who taught me basic dressage; Chico, a hardworking Quarter Horse and trail-riding partner; patient Mandy, who helped me learn the fine points of dressage; and Teddy, a Tennessee Walking horse, who carries me dependably now, when my eyes don't always focus well.

If you've picked up this book, you probably love horses too. Do you wonder, though, how horses can help you learn about God or deal with things like too much homework or relationships with friends? They can, because most horses are kind and gentle, intelligent and attuned to our moods. They hear our smallest whisper and respond to our lightest touch. They're patient and forgiving, encouraging us to be more like that too. Their temperament, as well as their beauty and talent, reflects the goodness and love of our Creator, helping us know God, others, and ourselves better.

I once watched a mare doing a dressage test with a foal at her side. When the rider urged the mare to canter a circle, the foal cantered close beside its mother. When the mare slowed to a trot or turned, so did her foal. It was so much fun to watch them. The beauty and talent of the mare was amazing, as was the close bond between her and her foal. This early bond protects the foal and helps it learn all the things young horses need to know.

As you read these devotions, have fun learning about horses. While you do, I pray you'll want to stay as close to Jesus as a foal does with its mother. He'll take you on amazing adventures each day, showing you how much he loves you and that the bond between you and him will never ever break. He'll always be beside you, protecting you and helping you become the loving and talented creation he desires you to be.

Kathryn O'Neill

Introduction

HOOFPRINTS OF HOPE is a collection of fifty-two devotions that will lead you on an adventurous trail ride with God. In part 1, "Breeds of Horses," you'll learn about fascinating breeds like the Appaloosa—a talented and colorful horse developed by the Nez Percé, a Native American tribe—and the Shire—a large draft breed now gaining popularity as a riding horse. In part 2, "Famous and Not-So-Famous Horses," you'll read about special horses like Sunny Jim, a bookmobile horse who brought stories to remote locations, and Seabiscuit, a racehorse who overcame failure with the help of a patient trainer. Part 3, "God Made Horses Special," explains how God designed the details of horses' bodies, such as their 360-degree range of vision and their ability to sleep while standing up. Lastly, in part 4, "Activities with Horses," you'll find out all about gymkhana and other fun activities you can do with horses, as well as the tack and equipment needed to ride and care for them.

A good trail has signs along the way to help you discover important ideas and insights. Think of each *Hoofprints* devotion as a stop along the trail, complete with fun information about horses and important spiritual truths about God, other people, and yourself. Here are several "signs" (or special features) to guide you on your trail ride as you read your devotion for the day:

A Bible verse will help you begin thinking about what God wants you to learn in the devotion.

"CORRAL YOUR THOUGHTS" provides one or more journaling questions with lines for you to write on.

"GALLOP INTO ACTION" nudges you to put what you've learned into action in your daily life.

"FUN NOTES FROM THE BARN" offers interesting facts about horses to share with friends and family.

At the end of the trail, you'll find two more features to make your ride more enjoyable.

Glossary of Horse Terms: In each devotion, you'll find horse-related words in **bold letters**. Turn to the glossary for definitions of these terms (see page 221).

Learn More: Keep learning about horses with this page of recommended books and websites (see page 235).

PART 1

Breeds of Horses

THROUGHOUT MOST OF HISTORY, horses carried people to settle new lands and then helped with whatever work needed to be done there. Plowing fields and hauling wagons called for big, strong horses, but riding horses needed to be lighter and faster. So people began breeding horses for different needs. Today there are about two hundred recognized horse and pony breeds. In this section, you'll discover the beauty and unique traits of twelve of those breeds—from ancient ones like the Caspian to modern breeds like the Gypsy Vanner.

1

APPALOOSAS

Seeing Spots

If we claim we have no sin, we are only fooling ourselves and not living in the truth. But if we confess our sins to him, he is faithful and just to forgive us our sins and to cleanse us from all wickedness.

1 JOHN 1:8-9

• • • • • • • • • •

IN AUGUST OF 1805, when the Lewis and Clark expedition reached the foot of the Rocky Mountains in what is today called Montana, Captain Lewis hiked to the top of Lemhi Pass. The expedition had spent over a year struggling up the Missouri River by boat. They had met Native people and discovered new animals like prairie dogs and grizzly bears. Now at the top of the pass, Lewis saw mountains stretching to the horizon, and he knew they needed horses to get to the Pacific Ocean. They traded with the Shoshone[1] tribe for horses to ride over those almost-endless mountain ranges.

When Lewis and Clark finally made it over all the mountains, they met the Nez Percé[2] people of what is today eastern Oregon. Lewis made a special entry in his journal about the fine spotted horses

1. The Shoshone people call themselves Neme or Newe.
2. The name *Nez Percé* is French for "pierced nose." Historically, the Nez Percé tribe have called themselves the Nimiipuu.

of the Nez Percé. He realized these horses were different from horses he'd seen with other tribes. The Nez Percé crossed those rugged mountain ranges twice every year—spending winters in Oregon and summers on the plains. So they bred their horses to be hardy and sure-footed (to safely travel mountain trails) and speedy (to hunt buffalo on the plains).

In wars with the United States **cavalry** in the late 1800s, many Nez Percé spotted horses were lost or destroyed when the tribe was forced to settle on a reservation. But in the 1930s, people in Oregon gathered descendants of the spotted horses from wild **herds** and ranches and began to revive the breed. Today, **Appaloosas**—probably named for the Palouse region of Oregon—are popular riding horses in both Western and English activities.

Appaloosas come in beautiful patterns. Some look dusted with white, sporting what's called a snowflake pattern. Leopard Appaloosas have small spots all over. On others, it looks like a white blanket covers the horse's hindquarters, either solid white or spotted. Breeders never know which pattern will show up on **foals**.

Spots on Appaloosas are beautiful, but some spots, like dirt and stains, are not. The Bible sometimes compares our sins to the not-so-good kind of spots.

We may not want to admit that we sin, but things like lying or unkind actions and words leave ugly spots on us that separate us from God. Thankfully, when you recognize you have sinned and confess it to God, he forgives you for Jesus' sake and washes away your spots.

CORRAL YOUR THOUGHTS: Think back over your week. Did you say anything unkind to anyone, such as a classmate, friend, or family member? Did you disobey a parent or caretaker? On the lines below, write about how you might speak differently if you could do it over.

GALLOP INTO ACTION: If you've said something you regret, ask God to forgive you. Then go and ask forgiveness from the person you sinned against.

FUN NOTES FROM THE BARN: Many Appaloosas that have dark-colored legs without white markings such as socks or stockings have vertical stripes on their hooves.

2

ARABIANS

A Beautiful Wind from the Desert

God created human beings in his own image. In the image of God he created them; male and female he created them.

GENESIS 1:27

TODAY'S PUREBRED ARABIAN HORSE has changed little from the desert horse Bedouin tribesmen of the Middle East rode thousands of years ago. No one knows the origin of **Arabians**, but the Bedouin treasured these horses with their elegant heads that taper to small **muzzles**. Large dark eyes, small ears, and **dished profiles** add to the unique look of Arabians. These horses are unique in other ways too. They have one less vertebra in their spines and one less pair of ribs, making their backs shorter than other horses. With their gracefully arched necks and flying manes and tails, they **galloped** with the wind out of the desert to become known all over the world.

But beauty isn't the only thing Arabians have. The Bedouin bred their horses with large hearts and lungs to give them great speed and endurance for the harsh desert climate. The Bedouin loved their horses so much that they often kept them in their own tents, creating an affectionate, intelligent, and loyal horse.

When Crusaders in the Middle Ages returned from the wars, some brought the talented Arabian horse back with them. Europeans then began crossbreeding them with their native horses, which improved those breeds. Today, almost all **Thoroughbred** horses trace their ancestry back to one of three Arabian **stallions** brought to England in the 1600s and 1700s. The Arabians gave speed and heart to the Thoroughbred breed. Another two Arabian stallions were important in the breeding of the famous white **Lipizzan** horses. **Purebred** Arabians have a superpower of passing many of their good traits to other types of horses, and today their genes show up in every breed of riding horse. What's most important, though, is that Arabians have also passed on to other horses their great heart and gentle and loyal nature.

The Bible says that when God created human beings, he created them in his image. That doesn't mean your physical looks, although God did create everything about you, from your hair color to your ten toes. What *is* meant is that you are created with an inner beauty like God. Just as Arabian horses have passed on many of their beautiful traits to other horses, so God shares many of his traits with his people. You are wonderfully made by the God of all creation, blessed with amazing talents like creativity, honesty, compassion, intelligence, and the ability to love God and others.

CORRAL YOUR THOUGHTS: Use your journaling lines to list some of the beautiful inner talents and personality traits God has given you.

GALLOP INTO ACTION: Think of a way to use one of those good talents to help a friend or family member this week. Then go do it!

FUN NOTES FROM THE BARN: Can you imagine riding one hundred miles over mountains in just twenty-four hours? The Tevis Cup in California is a hundred-mile mountain endurance race that's been challenging horses and riders for almost seventy years. Sixty of its winners have ridden Arabian horses, whose large hearts and lungs gave them the stamina to win.

3

CASPIANS

Lost and Found

If a man has a hundred sheep and one of them wanders away, what will he do? Won't he leave the ninety-nine others on the hills and go out to search for the one that is lost? . . . In the same way, it is not my heavenly Father's will that even one of these little ones should perish.

MATTHEW 18:12, 14

ABOUT FIVE HUNDRED YEARS before Jesus was born, King Darius I—the Persian king who aided the Israelites in rebuilding the Temple—ruled a huge kingdom that stretched across the Middle East. Wall carvings on the ruins of his palace at Persepolis, in today's Iran, show Darius in a chariot pulled by tiny horses. People in other carvings in the ruins are riding such small horses that the riders' feet touch the ground.

The Persian kingdom fell long ago, and the tiny horses were thought to be extinct until 1965, when Louise Firouz, an American living in Iran, began looking for small horses for children at her riding school. In the mountains of northern Iran near the

Caspian Sea, she saw a small stallion pulling a heavy cart. The stallion, named Ostad, didn't plod along like most workhorses. He trotted and frisked through the town with his mane and tail streaming out like a banner.

Louise was familiar with the carvings at Persepolis and believed she'd found that lost breed. She bought Ostad and searched for others like him. Soon she had a small herd of what she named **Caspians**, for the large, nearby inland sea. Caspians are pony size, but they look like small, elegant Arabian horses. And like Arabians, Caspians are smart and friendly. They have large eyes and silky manes and tails. They're strong at pulling loads but also have smooth **gaits** for riding.

Research by archaeologists and zoologists, as well as genetic testing, has shown that Caspians are an ancient breed of horses, even older than Arabians. Louise Firouz may well have found horses descended from the lost horses pictured on the walls of Darius's palace.

Powerful Persian kings once treasured the little Caspian horses, but when the Persian empire fell, the horse was lost for 1,300 years. Sometimes you may feel small and lost, forgotten like the Caspian horses. But remember that the powerful King of all the universe treasures you and sent his Son, the Good Shepherd, to search for you. Jesus doesn't want even one of his little ones to be lost. And when Jesus finds you, he will never lose you, because his Kingdom is forever and so is his love for you.

CORRAL YOUR THOUGHTS: Are there times when you feel a little lost, like people don't really see you? Write about it on the lines below.

GALLOP INTO ACTION: Use a three-by-five card to write down Matthew 18:12 and 14. Then memorize it to remind yourself that your Father in heaven treasures you and always watches over you.

FUN NOTES FROM THE BARN: Horses and ponies are measured from their hooves up to their withers (the ridge where the horse's shoulders meet) in a unit called hands (the width of an adult's hand, or 4 inches). Caspians stand only 10 to 12 hh (hands high), or 40 to 48 inches, so some people think they're ponies, but Caspians are true horses.

4

AMERICAN CURLIES

Horses of a Different Coat

Thank you for making me so wonderfully complex! Your workmanship is marvelous—how well I know it.

PSALM 139:14

AMERICAN CURLY HORSES (sometimes called Bashkir Curly horses) look different from other horses. Their winter coats feel like a fleece blanket. Patting them is like running your hand through lambswool or the hair of a poodle. Even the hair inside their ears is curly, and their eyelashes curl upward instead of sweeping downward like other horses' eyelashes. American Curly horse manes are thick and often look like they've just been unbraided.

Most Curlies shed out to a thinner, less curly coat in the summer. Unlike other horses, they may shed part or all of their manes and tails too. But once cold weather returns, their hair grows back thick and curly.

No one knows how curly-coated horses came to North America. Some believe they came with early Russian settlers to the Pacific coast region, but ship records don't list any horses on board. The first proven records of Curly horses in North America are Native American drawings. A Lakota buffalo hide from 1801 shows curly-coated horses.

In 1898, a Nevada rancher and his son saw three curly-coated horses in a **mustang** band. They captured them and discovered that these unique horses made talented and hardworking ranch horses that could survive the cold temperatures of prairie winters. Today, Curly horses do well in many events, including endurance riding and Western sports.

Though Curly horses are different, they fit well into any herd of horses, but for humans, it's sometimes hard to feel different. Are you taller than your classmates, or does your family have different customs and foods than your neighbors? Perhaps you've moved to a new school, and your clothes don't look like what others are wearing. Everyone wants to belong, but your differences might make you feel self-conscious or left out.

When you are lonely, you can talk to Jesus, who grew up just like you and understands it's tough to be different. Remember, you'll always be a part of

Jesus' herd, and you can trust that God knew what he was doing when he made marvelous you.

CORRAL YOUR THOUGHTS: Have you ever felt different or left out? Write a letter to God, telling him about it below.

GALLOP INTO ACTION: Do you know someone who is new to your school or often left out? Invite them to join you and your friends at lunch or in a study group.

FUN NOTES FROM THE BARN: The origin of the American Curly horse remains a mystery, but it's no mystery that most Curlies have a gentle nature and a love for people.

5

GYPSY VANNERS

Equine Stars

Love is patient and kind. Love is not jealous.

1 CORINTHIANS 13:4

GYPSY VANNER HORSES SEEM to have it all—beautiful colors and long, flowing manes and tails. Long hair called feathering grows on their lower legs. When the horses trot or canter, the feathering swirls around, making it look like the horses are dancing. When Gypsy Vanners were first introduced to Americans at the Kentucky Horse Park in 1998, they caused a sensation. Today, people still crowd around them as if they are movie stars.

The Gypsy Vanner breed was developed after World War II by several groups of Roma people in the United Kingdom. People once thought the Roma came from Egypt, so they used to call them Gypsies, but this term is now considered offensive to the Roma. In fact, historians today believe the Roma people lived long ago in northern India and gradually migrated westward. By the late Middle Ages, they lived all over Europe, but they seldom settled down on farms or in cities like most people. They remained nomadic—living in tents and moving with the seasons. The Roma were known everywhere for their love of color and music and their horses.

In more modern times, some Roma began to live and travel in horse-drawn wagons called caravans. These looked a little like the covered wagons of American pioneer days. In the United Kingdom, the Roma decorated their wagons with colorful patterns. At first, they used many types of horses to pull their wagons, but some Roma wanted to breed a small and beautiful horse to go with their colorful caravans. Over the years, they blended strong workhorses like Shires, Clydesdales, and Friesians with some of Britain's sturdy native ponies. Gradually, the Roma developed the Gypsy Vanner horses of today. These horses are strong and beautiful but also gentle and easily trained for riding or harnessing.

Have you ever felt jealous of a classmate? Someone you thought was more beautiful or handsome than you, who seemed more like a star because they had more talents or better clothes? It's hard not to feel jealous, especially when other people pay more attention to them than to you—just like when people flocked to see the Gypsy Vanners over other horses. The Lord understands when you envy others, but he calls his children to love others. That may seem impossible, but remember, biblical love is not just a feeling. It's about actions—how you treat someone, even someone you may not like very much. With God's help, you can begin to turn your jealousy into ways to show Christian love.

CORRAL YOUR THOUGHTS: What are some traits or gifts you envy in others? On the journaling lines below, write a letter to God about your feelings.

GALLOP INTO ACTION: Gypsy Vanner horses show their love for people by being gentle and kind. Think of three kind things you could do to show love for someone you envy.

FUN NOTES FROM THE BARN: A horse called The Gypsy King was one of the first Gypsy Vanner stallions to come to the US, arriving in 1998. "Bill," as he was then called, had black-and-white pinto markings and was one of the most photographed Gypsy Vanner horses. A company called Breyer even made a model of him.

6

ICELANDIC HORSES

A Smooth Ride

God has given each of you a gift from his great variety of spiritual gifts. Use them well to serve one another.

1 PETER 4:10

• • • • • • • • • •

MOST HORSES HAVE FOUR gaits. A gait is the way a horse moves. These gaits include the walk, trot, canter, and gallop. Of the four, the trot is usually the bumpiest, so English riders often post, or rise up and down in the saddle, to make it more comfortable. Western riders slow the trot down to a smoother jog. Posting gets tiring, though, and a jog is still bumpy, so many people enjoy riding a gaited horse. A gaited horse has one or more extra gaits. One of these—the running walk—is smooth but covers ground as fast as a trot.

Paso Finos and Tennessee Walking horses are just two of the many breeds of gaited horses, but one of the most interesting gaited breeds is the Icelandic horse. In the late ninth century AD, Vikings from Norway and the British Isles discovered Iceland and settled it. They brought horses with them for transportation and to work on their farms. Iceland is remote, and soon, Icelanders stopped importing any new horses—in fact, no new horses have been allowed into Iceland for a thousand years. That means Icelandic horses living in Iceland are a very pure breed because they haven't been crossbred with any other breed.

Until recently Icelandic horses grew up in free-roaming herds. Iceland is a volcanic land that had few roads before the late 1800s, so these sure-footed horses were the only means of transportation. Icelandic horses come in over a hundred colors, including pinto patterns, and their double coats provide protection from cold and snowy winters. These horses are small—just 12 to 14 hh (48 to 56 inches)—but they can carry an adult rider over long distances in a high-stepping running walk called the tolt. All Icelandic horses are born with this gait, which is smoother than a trot but just as fast.

Icelanders love their talented gaited horses that smoothly carry them over bumpy lands. God loves you and has given you special talents that may help smooth out the bumps in a friend or family member's day. If mornings are rushed, you might help your mom or dad get a younger sibling ready for school. Or if you have a talent for math or science, you could help a friend study for tests in those subjects. If you like dogs, you could walk a neighbor's dog. Whatever your special gift is, don't neglect to use it to help others.

CORRAL YOUR THOUGHTS: Do you know someone who needs some help? Use the lines below to make a plan to help them.

GALLOP INTO ACTION: Like the Icelandic horse, you don't have to be big to help someone. Use some of your talents to smooth out a bump in the life of a friend or family member today.

FUN NOTES FROM THE BARN: Some Icelandic horses have another special gait called the pace. In the pace, the legs on the same side of the horse move together in a gait similar to a trot but almost as fast as a gallop.

7

LIPIZZANS

Schooling for Airs Above the Ground

Intelligent people are always ready to learn. Their ears are open for knowledge.

PROVERBS 18:15

DO YOU FEEL LIKE you have to spend lots of time in school? Horse training is often called schooling, and one breed of horse, called Lipizzans (or Lipizzaners), spends lots of time in school too. Long ago, Spanish people bred Lipizzan-type horses from Spanish and North African horses. These horses got their high-set tails and large eyes from their desert ancestors. Their shorter legs and muscular bodies and necks came from Spanish horses. The combination gave them the control and balance needed for the activity of dressage.

In the 1500s, rulers of the Habsburg Empire brought many Lipizzan-type horses to Austria for their riding school and started breeding farms there. Lipizzan horses are now bred all over the world, but the most famous are still those that perform at the Spanish Riding School in Vienna, Austria.

Those exciting performances couldn't happen without the careful schooling that starts right from the beginning of a foal's life. At the school's breeding farm, foals are weaned at six months. They then join a foal herd for another six months. When they're a year old, they run and play with other yearlings on mountain pastures to develop hardiness and surefootedness. When they turn four, Lipizzans begin their schooling to become carriage horses or perform at the riding school.

The stallions chosen to join the performances spend about six more years in school. They must learn the skills of dressage, which include piaffe—trotting in place—and canter pirouettes. In a canter pirouette the horse moves in a small circle, pivoting around its inside back hoof. They're schooled at a pace that's good for each horse, and most join performances when they're about ten. Under the chandeliers of the beautiful riding hall, groups of four or more horses "dance" in unison to music. A few horses remain in school even longer to learn more advanced movements called "airs above the ground." One of the most difficult is the capriole, in which the horse leaps up into the air and kicks out with its hind legs.

Gentle and eager-to-learn Lipizzans amaze their audiences. Your heavenly Father has given you an even greater responsibility—to learn skills to care for the people and creatures of his world. Whether he calls you to care for a home and family, to teach, to keep people healthy, or to sing and dance on a stage, your schooling will help you do amazing work. And you'll do your job in the most beautiful "hall" of all—God's world.

CORRAL YOUR THOUGHTS: What would you like to do when you grow up? Write some of your dreams below.

GALLOP INTO ACTION: Decide to be an eager learner like a Lipizzan and pray that God will help you find the best ways to care for his world today and in the future.

FUN NOTES FROM THE BARN: Lipizzan foals are born brown or gray, but most lighten to light gray when they're between six and ten years old and become even whiter-looking as they age.

8

MUSTANGS

Digging Deep

They delight in the law of the Lord, meditating on it day and night.

PSALM 1:2

BY THE BEGINNING OF the twentieth century, about two million mustangs roamed the ranges of the western United States. Modern horses aren't native to North or South America, so where did they come from? They came by ship with Spanish explorers in the 1500s. Over time, some horses escaped and formed herds of—not wild—but feral horses. A feral horse is one that was once domesticated (tame) or that is descended from escaped domesticated horses. The word *mustang* comes from the Spanish word *mestengo*, meaning "wild" or "stray."

Gradually horses migrated north and south and were captured by Native tribes. By the 1700s, horses had reached the Nez Percé tribe in today's Oregon and the Lakota and Cheyenne tribes of the northern Great Plains. Horses transformed the lives of Native Americans. They could hunt buffalo more successfully, travel greater distances, and make war among themselves and with settlers. But their horses also often escaped and joined roving mustang bands.

As settlers and ranchers from the East moved in, they brought their own horses and cattle. US President Teddy Roosevelt, who owned a ranch in North Dakota in the late 1800s, wrote about the open prairies where herds of wild horses competed with cattle for grazing. With few fences to hold them, tame horses easily joined wild herds. Mustang **stallions** would also swoop in to steal a settler's **mares**. In this way, all but the most isolated mustang herds have become a mixture of many types of horses.

One thing all mustangs have in common, though, is the intelligence and hardiness to adapt to different environments, from prairies to forested mountains to dry deserts. Unlike cattle, horses know how to dig through snow to find grass to eat. And horses can smell water underground, so in the desert or during times of little rain, they'll dig down until they find water to satisfy their thirst.

God has given mustangs unique abilities to survive difficult conditions. He's given you a desire to know him. And when you dig deep into the Bible, you'll find food to grow your trust in your heavenly

Father, who knows all your needs. Jesus promises that the living water of his Word will refresh you when you're feeling tired or troubled. Best of all, his Word leads to eternal life.

CORRAL YOUR THOUGHTS: Every part of the Bible has food for your soul. Which book would you like to dig into? Pick a chapter or passage to read and write what you learn below.

GALLOP INTO ACTION: A herd of mustangs may dig together to clear an area of snow. Ask a friend or two to meet to study the Bible with you.

FUN NOTES FROM THE BARN: With good training most mustangs make good riding horses. Every so often, the United States' Wild Horse and Burro Program rounds some up for adoption, which helps keep wild mustang numbers down to around thirty thousand.

9

PINTOS AND PAINTS

Colorful and Confusing Patterns

He [Jesus] calls his own sheep by name. . . . I am the good shepherd; I know my own sheep.

JOHN 10:3, 14

WHAT'S THE DIFFERENCE BETWEEN paints and pintos? You're not alone if you're unsure. And you may have other questions: Can they be any color? Are there different kinds of patterns? Can two paints or pintos have the same pattern? Is an Appaloosa a paint?

Paints and pintos look alike when it comes to coat colors and patterns. But there is one important difference between them. Paints are a breed of colored horses that must also have Quarter Horses or Thoroughbreds as parents. Pintos are a color breed. Since pinto patterns show up in many breeds, the pinto registry accepts horses of any breed, as well as ponies and miniature horses. Lastly, Appaloosas are a separate breed. Their unique kind of spotting is neither paint nor pinto.

Paints and pintos have the same types of coat

patterns. A tobiano horse is covered with round or oval white markings, and they usually have white legs and two-colored tails. Their heads are dark and may have blazes and stars like solid-colored horses. Their coats may be mostly white or mostly dark-colored in a variety of colors—from bay or black to chestnut, palomino, or buckskin.

Horses with the overo pattern, which is less common, are dark with jagged white patches that rarely go across the back. It may even look like someone splashed white paint onto a dark-colored horse. Unlike tobianos, overos often have dark legs but may have lots of white on their faces. One or both eyes may be blue, and the tail of an overo is usually just one color.

When you first look at a herd of paints or pintos, it looks confusing. You may wonder if even their owners can pick out their horses from the herd. But no two paints or pintos are exactly alike. The Bible says you are unique, too, and wonderfully made by God. There's no one exactly like you, and Jesus, the Good Shepherd, knows your name and loves you. No matter how big a herd . . . er, crowd, you're in, he'll never lose you or confuse you with someone else.

CORRAL YOUR THOUGHTS: What does it mean to you that Jesus knows your name? Write your thoughts below.

GALLOP INTO ACTION: At the top of a piece of paper, write *Jesus Knows Me*. Then divide the paper into three columns. Label one column *My Favorite Things*, another *My Talents*, and a third *My Dreams*. Fill in each column, remembering that Jesus knows you and loves you.

FUN NOTES FROM THE BARN: A rare pattern called tovero combines the tobiano and overo patterns. These horses are mostly all white with color just on their ears and heads. Native Americans prized them and called them medicine hat or war bonnet horses.

10

QUARTER HORSES

Hard Workers Everywhere

Work willingly at whatever you do, as though you were working for the Lord rather than for people.

COLOSSIANS 3:23

DID YOU KNOW Quarter Horses started out as race-horses in colonial America? There were no racetracks, but people used village streets or level pastures to race their riding horses in short quarter-mile races or sprints. Their horses were often mixtures of Spanish horses from Florida and early Thoroughbreds. The fastest of these horses were called Celebrated American Quarter Running Horses. Their heavily muscled hindquarters shot them forward into the lead during sprints.

When Americans headed west in the 1800s, they took their calm and willing Quarter Horses with them. These all-around horses pulled the pioneers' wagons and herded livestock on western farms and ranches.

After the Civil War, people in eastern cities and crews laying the many new railroad lines began to demand more beef. To meet the demand, ranchers went to Texas, where wild longhorn cattle were free to whoever could round them up and herd them north to railroad shipping depots. These long, dusty cattle drives became legends of the American West, and the horse that kept the cattle moving on the drives was the Quarter Horse. It could sprint out after a straying longhorn and then turn on a dime to chase it back into the herd.

The American Quarter Horse, as it's known today, still has what ranchers call "cow sense." That's the ability to read a cow's body language and herd it to the correct place. Today Quarter Horses excel in many activities, but no matter what they're asked to do, they give it their best. Their calm and willing spirit make them one of the best all-around horses and a favorite with people all over the world.

Sometimes you may not want to do schoolwork or help with chores at home, but God calls us to work hard at whatever job we're given, just like the eager Quarter Horse. When Jesus was about your age, the Bible says he grew in wisdom, stature, and favor with God and all people, and you can too. When you're willing to tackle the work given to you and do your best, God and your teachers, family, and friends will know they can depend on you.

CORRAL YOUR THOUGHTS: Do you glorify God with your best effort in schoolwork and chores? Use your journaling lines to complete the "Gallop into Action" activity below.

GALLOP INTO ACTION: Make a list of your school subjects and chores. Draw smiley faces next to ones you work hard on and frowny faces next to any you speed through too quickly. Work hard like a Quarter Horse to turn those frowny faces into smiley ones this week.

FUN NOTES FROM THE BARN: Ranch tasks that require separating a cow from the herd or roping one for branding or vaccinations have also become events at Western shows.

11

SHETLANDS

Patient Ponies

The Holy Spirit produces this kind of fruit in our lives: love, joy, peace, patience, kindness, goodness, faithfulness, gentleness, and self-control.

GALATIANS 5:22-23

SHETLAND PONIES, ONE OF the smallest pony breeds, are native to islands off the north coast of Scotland called the Shetland Islands. These cold and windy islands, with few trees, lie just a few hundred miles south of the Arctic Circle. The harsh climate helped shape Shetland ponies into a strong, hardy breed. Shetlands come in many colors, from blacks and browns to bays, chestnuts, and even pintos. No matter what color they are, Shetland ponies, with their thick tails and manes and bushy forelocks tumbling down over their eyes, look a little like big sheepdogs.

Shetland ponies have lived on their islands since ancient times. For their size, Shetlands are one of the strongest equines, and they helped the islanders farm their land and haul heavy loads. In the

1700s, because people needed coal to power all the new machines of the Industrial Revolution, mines opened all over Great Britain and the United States. Thousands of small Shetland ponies worked underground in the mines, hauling coal out of low tunnels. Many Shetland ponies spent their entire lives underground, until machines finally took over.

After World War I, people discovered that Shetlands also made quiet and gentle riding ponies for children. Now Shetland ponies have a new challenge. They must stand patiently while children hug and kiss them. They help children, who may be too loud or too wiggly, learn to ride. Other breeds of horses and ponies often don't have the patience for this.

Shaggy Shetland ponies may not be beautiful on the outside, but their kind and gentle inner nature has helped them work patiently on island farms, in deep mines, and with brand-new little riders. Sometimes, classmates or younger brothers and sisters can be too loud, get in your way, be really messy, or break your favorite things. When that happens, remember that the Holy Spirit lives in you and that you can ask him to help you be kind and gentle like a patient Shetland pony.

CORRAL YOUR THOUGHTS: Do you have a classmate or younger brother or sister who makes it hard for you to be patient? Write your thoughts about what patience looks like on your journaling lines.

GALLOP INTO ACTION: Pray and ask the Holy Spirit to help you find ways to be more patient. Perhaps you could find time to play with a younger sibling or share a snack with a classmate.

FUN NOTES FROM THE BARN: The classic Shetland pony is about 40 inches, or a little more than the height of a yardstick. Some modern Shetlands are larger and more elegant looking.

12

SHIRES

Big and Strong

[God] takes no pleasure in the strength of a horse or in human might. No, the LORD's delight is in those who fear him, those who put their hope in his unfailing love.

PSALM 147:10-11

ONE OF THE TALLEST and heaviest horses ever was Sampson. Born in England in 1846, Sampson was over seven feet tall at the withers. And he weighed over one and a half tons. That's more than some small cars. His owners changed his name to Mammoth, and he went down in the record books.

Shire horses like Mammoth are native to the central counties, or shires, of England. These mostly black, bay, or gray workhorses have a long history of using their patient strength to help people with different jobs. No one is sure of the breed's exact origins, but experts agree that ancestors of the Shire horses were the tanks of medieval warfare. Their great size and power carried knights in heavy armor—often at a combined weight of around four hundred pounds—into battle.

In time warfare changed, and so did the work of Shires. People discovered that these horses could help with farmwork and transportation. So by the 1800s, gentle Shires pulled plows to ready fields for planting. They hauled wagons loaded with fuel and food through cities, and they pulled coaches packed with people along rough dirt roads.

Then along came trucks and tractors. Few people needed the Shires' strength anymore, and soon there were only a few thousand left in the world. Even their great strength and endurance couldn't help the Shires. But Shire breed associations and other groups love the Shires—with their mammoth patience and power—and encourage Shire breeders and owners through education, exhibitions, and competitions. Shires also keep on learning new skills, like becoming riding horses, and that brings hope that this unique breed will survive.

Like Shire horses, we often need to learn new skills. We may think we can learn to play a musical instrument or swim the butterfly stroke in our own strength, but new skills can be hard. You may get discouraged and want to give up. But instead of depending on your own strength, turn to God for help. He delights to give you the patience and strength to keep going and learn new things.

CORRAL YOUR THOUGHTS: What new skill would you like to learn? Write a prayer on your journaling lines, asking God to help you.

GALLOP INTO ACTION: Breaking a skill down into smaller chunks makes it easier to learn. List some of the steps needed for a new skill and ask God to give you mammoth strength and patience to keep learning step-by-step, just like a Shire horse.

FUN NOTES FROM THE BARN: Throughout history horses powered everything from the mills used to grind wheat to the wagons that carried the flour to market. So when machines came along, the term *horsepower* helped people understand how much work the new engines could do. Horsepower is still the unit used to measure the power of machines like cars and trucks.

PART 2

Famous and Not-So-Famous Horses

IN THIS SECTION you'll meet fourteen extraordinary horses. Some starred in movies and television. Others overcame obstacles to become sports heroes. Four brave horses played important parts in history. Several of the horses survived hard times to help others, and a couple horses found fame in books. As you read these horses' stories, they may sometimes make you cry and sometimes laugh—but all of them will amaze you.

type of range mares are said to produce the ideal cow

reputation made by the First Vermont Cavalry in the
s a matter of record. This regiment was mounted on

FIG. 15.—Glittering Glory. Morgan saddle gelding

ses, and official reports made to the War Department
the horses in this organization stood the hardships of

13

FIGURE

Small but Mighty | *late 1700s*

Don't let anyone think less of you because you are young. Be an example to all believers in what you say, in the way you live, in your love, faith, and your purity.

1 TIMOTHY 4:12

DO YOU KNOW WHAT the state horse of Massachusetts is? Or the state animal of Vermont? They're both the Morgan horse. Morgans were one of the first truly American horse breeds, and they could do it all. As the United States grew, Morgans hauled people and products over bumpy roads to connect its regions and states. Morgans went west with the pioneers to herd cattle on ranches or pull plows to turn grassland into farmland. And it all began with the birth of a small horse named Figure.

Not long after the American Revolutionary War, a music teacher, farmer, and businessman named Justin Morgan moved from Massachusetts to Vermont. Before he left, he received a bay colt named Figure from a farmer who owed him money. Figure didn't grow into a very big horse, so no one thought he could do much. But when Justin Morgan began loaning him out to neighbors, they discovered that Figure could easily haul logs to clear land and pull plows to plant crops. Justin Morgan began entering Figure in log-pulling contests, and he outpulled much bigger workhorses. Figure was fast too—outrunning Thoroughbreds in races.

When Justin Morgan died, Figure changed hands many times, continuing to work on farms, haul wagons, and march in parades. By then everyone wanted a colt or filly from the talented Justin Morgan horse. Figure passed on his kind nature, as well as his strength and speed, to all his foals. Other American breeds, such as Tennessee Walkers, Standardbreds, and Quarter Horses, have benefited from Morgan blood.

At first, Figure's small size fooled people into thinking he couldn't do much, but they soon found he could outwork and outrace much larger horses. Sometimes, when you're small or young, you might not think you can be a help to others. In the Bible, a young man called Timothy worried that he was too young to be helpful. But his friend Paul told Timothy that even though he was young, the way he spoke and lived would show he was a child of God and prove he could still serve others in a mighty way.

Figure's sons and daughters all inherited his mighty

talents and his ability to do whatever people asked him to do. You are made in the image of your heavenly Father, and he gives all his sons and daughters talents through the Holy Spirit. He'll make you strong to serve others, no matter how tall or small you are.

CORRAL YOUR THOUGHTS: Use your journaling lines to list three talents God has given you that could be helpful to others.

GALLOP INTO ACTION: Be like a mighty Morgan and surprise someone this week by using one of your talents to help them.

FUN NOTES FROM THE BARN: Because of their versatility, by the 1850s Morgan horses had become popular as workhorses, riding horses, and even stagecoach horses. Large numbers of Morgans became cavalry mounts. Today, Morgans do well in both Western and English riding activities as well as driving competitions.

THE AMERICAN PONY EXPRESS, EN ROUTE FROM THE MISSOURI RIVER TO SAN FRANCISCO.—FROM A D

when reading American
alifornia, Oregon, British
orth America contained in
d the questions naturally
it come from? where does
se, or a stagecoach, or a
nformation on this point,
cale of the pony express,
d also to get a view of it

munication between the
c and Pacific seaboards
ng them by railways have
time scarcely anything
. Between the Missouri
exists a huge wilderness
ge mountain-chains—the

Rocky and the Cascade Ranges. Through the whole of this must an Atlantic and Pacific railway be carried when it is made, if it be made through United States' territory. The railway works were extraordinary in perforating and climbing the Alleghanies. Railways are now being made through the mountains in India, and in other places where tremendous obstacles have to be overcome, yet on none of the lines made or being made do such formidable barriers exist as are found between the Atlantic and Pacific States of the American Union. The present unhappy state of affairs—the waste of war—is draining the national exchequer dry, and deferring to a distant date the completion of the most important work the United States' Government has had in hand since the declaration of independence—the binding their eastern and western territory together with a band of iron.

Mr. W. H. Russell, of the firm of Russell, Major, and Waddel, extensive Government contractors for the conveyance of stores overland to the States on the west side of the Rocky Mountains, having observed the daily-increasing importance of a more rapid means of communication than then existed, hit upon the exceedingly bold idea of running a pony express from the Missouri

River to the Pacific Ocean, carrying a telegram from New
part of the States, to San Francisco in eight days, and
Those who knew the country through which the express mu
heads, and said it would never do; the route was far north
the roads impassable, the snow lying often fifteen feet deep
then took 115 days to make a quick passage between N
Francisco.

Mr. Russell was not the man to set aside a plan he had
he could carry out by any multiplication of difficulties: he th
make the attempt. First he built stations all along the rout
well and plentifully, then engaged a corps of fearless and
and purchased about six hundred horses, the very best that m
Having done all this and a great deal more that was ne
1860, two ponies started simultaneously, one from San Fran
from St. Joseph, on the Missouri; and, although the season
able, the mud being in some places two or three feet d
distance, one thousand nine hundred miles, was run in sev

14

SYLPH

First Pony Express Horse | *1860–1861*

You are a letter from Christ. . . . This "letter" is not written with pen and ink, but with the Spirit of the living God . . . on human hearts.

2 CORINTHIANS 3:3

• • • • • • • • • •

A CANNON BOOMED OVERHEAD in celebration as Johnny Fry leaped into the saddle of his horse, Sylph. It was April 3, 1860, and they were the first horse and rider pair of the new Pony Express. Johnny and Sylph trotted through the streets of St. Joseph, Missouri, and boarded a ferry to cross the Missouri River. Once on the other side, they galloped to the first relay station on a route that stretched almost two thousand miles across mountains and deserts to California. They carried mail in the pockets of a specially designed leather covering called a *mochila*, which fit over the saddle.

The eighty young riders of the Pony Express came from all over the country. They had to be light in weight but brave and tough. The four hundred horses had to be tough, too, and fast. In the eastern sections of the route, many horses were former cavalry horses of Morgan and Thoroughbred breeding. In the West, lots of the horses were mustang crosses.

Each rider rode a hundred-mile route and changed horses every ten to fifteen miles at stations along their route. At the station, a fresh horse was already saddled, and riders had two minutes to transfer the mochila to the new horse, mount, and gallop on. The men and horses galloped day and night and in all weather. They followed wagon trails high over the Rockies in Wyoming. They pushed themselves and their horses through dry, scorching deserts in Nevada and survived blinding blizzards in the mountains leading down into California.

The Pony Express only lasted from April 1860 to October 1861, when the transcontinental, or cross-country, telegraph line was completed. But its brave men and horses carried important mail and news to California when the United States was on the brink of the Civil War. The three hundred thousand settlers and miners in California couldn't wait months or even weeks for news from the East.

The Lord has given you much more important news to take to people, and unlike the Pony Express riders, you don't have to climb mountains or brave deserts to do it. People who need the good news of Jesus Christ and his salvation live in your neighborhood and go to your school. The Bible says Christ has written his letter on your heart, so through your words and actions, you can show Christ's love to the people around you.

CORRAL YOUR THOUGHTS: Do you have a classmate or neighbor who needs to hear the good news of Jesus? Write some thoughts about what you'd like to share with them.

GALLOP INTO ACTION: Pray and ask Jesus to give you opportunities to be his love letter to them.

FUN NOTES FROM THE BARN: It usually took ten days for mail to reach California, but in March 1861, the Pony Express rode extra hard and fast to deliver a copy of President Lincoln's inaugural speech to California in just seven days and seventeen hours.

15

BLACK BEAUTY

Beloved Storybook Horse | *1870s*

The godly care for their animals.

PROVERBS 12:10

ANNA SEWELL, THE AUTHOR of *Black Beauty*, lived in the 1800s, when horses powered just about everything people did. In the country they trudged along canals pulling barges or carried people in fancy carriages. In cities horses clattered over cobblestone streets to deliver milk, coal, and food to city dwellers.

An accident when Anna was young made it hard for her to walk, so she got around in a horse-pulled cart. She loved horses and decided to write a story about them. In her book, Black Beauty is a gentle carriage and riding horse who tells the story of his life. All goes well until one night when a rider must gallop Black Beauty to and from the doctor during an emergency. When a tired and overheated Beauty gets back, a young, still-untrained groom named Joe tries to care for him but does all the wrong things, so Beauty gets sick. The heartbroken Joe watches and learns as the head groom nurses Beauty back to health.

Soon, the family moves, and Beauty is sold to a family that isn't as kind to their horses. As one of their carriage horses, he must wear a **bearing rein**, an uncomfortable type of **rein** that can pull horses' heads up so high that it can injure their necks. A careless rider also gallops Beauty over rough roads with a missing shoe, causing the horse to stumble and scar his knees. Beauty is then sold to several different places and is mistreated at each one, until a kind cabdriver in London buys him. Pulling a cab is hard work, but the cabdriver never overloads his cab, and he gives his horses Sundays off. But his next owners do overload their wagons, until Beauty finally collapses from overwork.

A young boy and his grandfather buy Beauty and nurse him back to health. Beauty becomes a carriage horse for three sisters. Their groom is none other than Joe, now grown into a kind and able horseman. Joe recognizes the gentle black horse he knew many years before. In the end, the ladies promise never to sell Black Beauty. He'll live a happy life, well cared for by Joe.

Anna Sewell loved horses and wrote *Black Beauty* to encourage people to treat horses with kindness. God lovingly created the world and its creatures and has given us the job of caring for it. His Word encourages those who have experienced his goodness to treat all the creatures of his world with kindness and gentleness.

CORRAL YOUR THOUGHTS: Do you have a favorite animal? Write down what you like about how God made that animal.

GALLOP INTO ACTION: Talk to a parent or caregiver about how you might practice caring for animals. Can you help with the family pet, put out seed for wild birds, or even volunteer with an animal rescue organization?

FUN NOTES FROM THE BARN: *Black Beauty* was the only book Anna Sewell ever wrote. It has sold millions of copies, and many believe it really did encourage people to treat horses with more kindness.

16

SUNNY JIM

A Horse Bookmobile | 1935–1943

Serve one another in love. For the whole law can be summed up in this one command: "Love your neighbor as yourself."

GALATIANS 5:13-14

• • • • • • • • • • •

SUNLIT LEAVES SPARKLED from an overnight rain as the book lady allowed her packhorse, Sunny Jim, to pick his way down the slippery bank into the creek. Earlier, she had stuffed Sunny Jim's saddlebags with fifty to one hundred books, destined for the mountain people of eastern Kentucky. Few roads led into the region, so the book lady and her horse often waded along creek beds up into the mountains. There they'd deliver the books to remote homes and schools. After a week, they'd pick up the books and replace them with new ones.

Sunny Jim was part of a program begun by American President Franklin Delano Roosevelt to help people get back to work during the Great Depression of 1929 to 1939. The Works Progress Administration (WPA) created jobs, mostly for men, to build schools, hospitals, and roads. First Lady Eleanor Roosevelt helped start another WPA program, the Pack Horse

Library Project. It employed about two hundred women to carry books by horseback to poor families in eastern Kentucky.

The project used local buildings as central libraries, but money for books was scarce. So people from other parts of Kentucky and around the country donated books and money to the new libraries. From the central libraries, women carried books on horses and mules, traveling over one hundred miles a week. The book ladies had to provide their own horses and care for them out of their monthly salary. Sunny Jim, along with other hardy horses and mules, carried books and riders up steep mountain paths that were often slippery with mud in the summer and ice in the winter.

When a book lady arrived at a backcountry home or school, children came running to see what books she had brought. Sometimes the lady would stay to visit and read aloud to the children and adults. The books and the visits brought joy and comfort into the lives of the mountain people and showed them how much they were loved.

You don't have to ride into remote mountains like Sunny Jim to see that there are needs everywhere. Jesus taught that the second greatest commandment was to love our neighbors as ourselves. When you show love for others and find ways to help them, you are like the ladies and horses of the Pack Horse Library Project, who showed true love to people in need.

CORRAL YOUR THOUGHTS: Write down several needs you have heard of in your school, church, or neighborhood.

GALLOP INTO ACTION: Talk with your family or friends to find ways to help someone in need this week.

FUN NOTES FROM THE BARN: By 1937 the Pack Horse librarians were serving fifty thousand families and 155 schools in the mountains of eastern Kentucky.

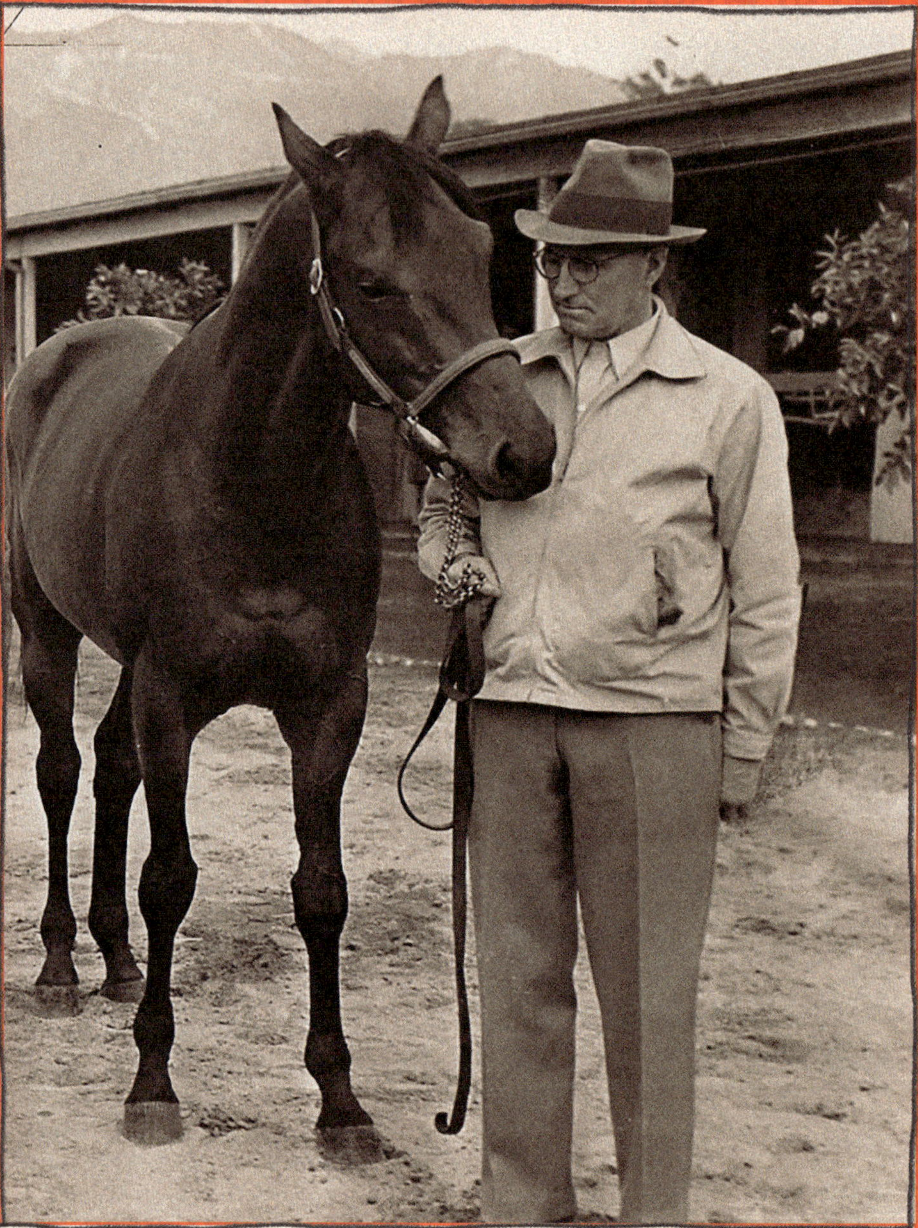

17

SEABISCUIT

Fame out of Failure | *1930s–1940s*

The Lord directs the steps of the godly. He delights in every detail of their lives. Though they stumble, they will never fall, for the Lord holds them by the hand.

PSALM 37:23-24

SEABISCUIT DIDN'T LOOK MUCH like a Thoroughbred racehorse. He was small, with a short wispy tail. He also had short legs with knobby knees that didn't completely straighten. When he galloped, he poked his left foreleg to the side before bringing it forward. Worst of all, Seabiscuit loved eating and sleeping more than racing.

His first trainer decided Seabiscuit was lazy and entered him in too many races for a young horse. The trainer allowed jockeys to whip Seabiscuit too much. By the time Seabiscuit was three years old, he'd won only a few races. He paced his stall instead of sleeping or eating. He had once been as friendly as a big dog, but now he began lunging at people when they passed his stall and fighting his handlers.

Tom Smith, a cowboy turned racehorse trainer, watched Seabiscuit race and saw he had promise.

But Tom also saw that Seabiscuit needed kindness to do his best. Tom's employer agreed to buy Seabiscuit. Tom gave the horse time to heal, and Seabiscuit began gaining weight and sleeping again. He started trusting people and followed Tom even without a lead rope. Tom chose a jockey for Seabiscuit named Johnny Pollard, who agreed that whipping wasn't the way to get Seabiscuit to run.

Seabiscuit was born in 1933 and raced during the Great Depression, when millions had lost jobs and were struggling to survive. So when Seabiscuit, a horse that had been failing, began to come from behind to win race after race, he caught the public's attention. People fell in love with the small racehorse with the scrawny tail and knobby knees. "The Biscuit" gave them hope that they could overcome their own hard times.

Because Seabiscuit's first trainer and jockeys didn't understand him, he failed over and over again. He stopped trying. But one kind trainer and jockey pair helped him become one of the most successful racehorses of all time.

Do you sometimes get discouraged when you fail at something? You may feel like quitting, but it's important to keep trying and doing your best. You may stumble sometimes, but you have an awesome

Helper who understands you better than Tom Smith understood Seabiscuit. Your heavenly Father, who holds all creation in his hands, holds *your* hand and will never let you fall.

CORRAL YOUR THOUGHTS: Have you ever felt like something you need to do is too hard? Write about something you're struggling with right now.

GALLOP INTO ACTION: Pray and ask God for help with whatever you're struggling with. If it's school related, you may want to ask a parent or caregiver for tutoring.

FUN NOTES FROM THE BARN: Racehorses race in age-groups, so on January 1 *every* horse born in a particular year moves up into the next age-group, no matter how early or late they were born. Since he was born in late May, Seabiscuit began his career racing against many horses that were five months older than he was.

18

SERGEANT RECKLESS

Courage Under Fire | *1950s–1960s*

God has not given us a spirit of fear and timidity, but of power, love, and self-discipline.

2 TIMOTHY 1:7

SMOKE SWIRLED AND ARTILLERY SHELLS exploded around her, but the little chestnut mare kept marching up the hill. It was 1950, and South Korea was under attack. Soldiers from South Korea, the United States, and several other nations fought as a united army to defend the country. Many battles took place on hills too steep for trucks, so marines had to carry up ammunition on their backs. That's when US Marine Corps Second Lieutenant Eric Pederson went looking for a horse and found a small racehorse called Flame of the Morning.

The marines renamed her Reckless and trained her to step over barbed wire and to kneel down when enemy shelling began. The first time Reckless heard the thunder of guns, she leaped straight up into the air. But she came down and stood her ground, because the marines had helped her overcome a horse's natural fear of loud noises. The marines loved the friendly little mare and let her share their

C rations (prepackaged meals) and their tents on winter nights.

Reckless carried ammunition for her marines in many battles. In one battle, she made fifty-one trips, delivering 386 heavy shells to gun crews on the ridges. Sometimes Reckless made the trip up the hill by herself and then carried wounded soldiers back down. Reckless was wounded twice, but she never quit.

After the war, Reckless came to the United States, and crowds of admirers and reporters greeted the heroic horse. She went to live at a marine base in Southern California, where she continued to support marines and their families. She made appearances to raise money for good causes. She welcomed marines and their family members who liked to visit and talk to her before deployments. And when veterans of the wars in Korea and Vietnam came to sit and talk, Reckless's gentle, friendly nature helped many feel a little better.

Reckless had to overcome her fears so that she could help the soldiers she loved. As you grow up, you'll need to learn new skills, like giving a speech or working a summer job. Your fears might tempt you not to even try. When you are afraid, remember that Jesus, who bravely faced the cross, has promised to give you power and love and self-discipline to face your fears, even in uphill battles.

CORRAL YOUR THOUGHTS: Are you ever afraid to try new things? Write down a new activity you would like to try, along with a prayer for courage to face your fear.

GALLOP INTO ACTION: Write 2 Timothy 1:7 on a card to keep in your Bible. Then memorize it to hold in your heart as you bravely face uphill battles, just like Reckless.

FUN NOTES FROM THE BARN: In 2013, the marines honored Reckless with a statue called *An Uphill Battle* at the marine training camp in Virginia. A bronze replica of Reckless trudges uphill, loaded down with ammunition.

19

TRIGGER

Television's Golden Horse | *1940s–1950s*

The laws of the Lord are true; each one is fair. They are more desirable than gold, even the finest gold.

PSALM 19:9-10

BEGINNING IN THE 1920S, movie stars began a tradition of putting their hand and footprints in squares of wet cement outside a famous Hollywood theater. In 1949, cameras flashed when a palomino horse named Trigger sank his hooves into the wet cement. Trigger was as much a star as his rider, Roy Rogers, a celebrated cowboy of Western movies and television.

The earliest movies were silent, and one of the first movies with sound was a Western. Its sound crew put a microphone in some sagebrush to catch the sound of horses galloping by. Audiences loved it, and many Westerns followed suit. Singing cowboys, along with their horses, starred in some of these. When Roy Rogers landed the lead role in one of the Westerns, he wanted a special horse that audiences would remember. As soon as he saw and rode the palomino stallion then named Golden Cloud, Roy fell in love with the calm and intelligent horse with the golden-tan coat.

Because Golden Cloud learned tricks quickly, they renamed him Trigger, and he and Roy went on to star in eighty-eight movies and one hundred television shows throughout the 1940s and 1950s. Trigger was a Thoroughbred cross with a wide blaze on his face and one white sock on his left hind leg. In movies, when he chased the bad guys, Trigger's snowy-white mane and tail flowed out on the wind. Publicity photos often showed the golden horse rearing, with Roy sitting in the saddle and waving. Trigger could hold that pose longer than most other horses. Roy loved Trigger so much he bought him for $2,500, which was a lot of money in those days, especially on his low beginning salary.

Roy Rogers treasured Trigger for the golden shine that helped the cowboy become a star. Millions of children loved Trigger and dreamed of riding a golden horse too. But Psalm 19 reminds us that God's Word is more desirable than gold, even the finest gold. God gave us his Word to teach us to love him and our neighbors. When you treasure God's Word, you may not become an earthly star like Roy Rogers or Trigger, but you'll discover much greater gold—eternal life with God, a gold that will never fade.

CORRAL YOUR THOUGHTS: What are three ways you can treasure God's Word in your life? Write about them on the journaling lines below.

GALLOP INTO ACTION: God sent his Son, the Living Word, to save us from our sins so we can have eternal life with him and to teach us how to live as his people. Read John 3:1-21 and put a star next to verses that explain how you may have eternal life. Talk to a parent or caregiver if you have questions.

FUN NOTES FROM THE BARN: Palomino coloring shows up in many breeds, so the palomino registry is a color breed association. That means they accept horses of any breed that have palomino coats—cream to dark-gold with dark eyes and light manes and tails.

20

BUTTERMILK

Not the Main Attraction | 1940s–1950s

[Jesus] sat down, called the twelve disciples over to him, and said, "Whoever wants to be first must take last place and be the servant of everyone else."

MARK 9:35

"ACTION!" YELLED THE DIRECTOR, and the Quarter Horse named Buttermilk shot forward. That's what he was good at, but Dale Evans reined him back, because she and Buttermilk had to let the stars of the show—Roy Rogers and his horse, Trigger—go first. Rogers and Trigger were wildly popular. Audiences loved when Roy and his golden palomino chased down the bad guys. But Roy needed a costar, and though Dale Evans, a well-known singer, couldn't ride, she was chosen to join the cast.

The horse trainers and handlers could provide gentle horses and teach Dale to ride. But no one could decide what color horse she should have. At first Dale rode a pinto, but its flashy looks took attention away from Trigger. Next they tried a gentle palomino named Pal, but Pal looked too much like Trigger. Finally, Glenn Randall, the horse trainer, discovered a small Quarter Horse named Soda on a Wyoming ranch. He brought Soda to California and tied him next to Trigger on the movie set. He wanted Dale and Roy to see the two horses together. Soda was a light-tan buckskin with a black mane and tail and black legs. Roy and Dale liked Soda and thought he'd be a great contrast to Trigger. Dale thought the horse looked like milky clouds, so Soda became Buttermilk.

Because they were the stars, Roy and Trigger got most of the attention, and other actors and horses had to play supporting roles. Buttermilk may not have liked letting Trigger go first in chases, but otherwise the two horses got along well. The buckskin Quarter Horse went on to support Trigger in the rest of his movies and television shows.

Like many people, you may not like playing a supporting or servant's role. Jesus' disciples certainly didn't. In the Gospel of Mark, they argued about which of them was the greatest. Jesus knew about their argument and called the disciples to him. He told them if they wanted to be great, they needed to have a servant's heart—not seeking to be first but to help others. When you get upset about not being first, remember that Jesus calls his children to put others ahead of themselves.

CORRAL YOUR THOUGHTS: Write about a time when you wanted to be first but someone else got to be first instead. Explain how you felt.

GALLOP INTO ACTION: Ask the Holy Spirit to help you have a servant's heart and find a way to help a friend or family member today.

FUN NOTES FROM THE BARN: In Western movies and television shows, many people worked behind the scenes. People called wranglers cared for all the horses, keeping them calm and getting them ready for their next scenes.

21

MISTY OF CHINCOTEAGUE

Braving the Storm | *late 1940s–1960s*

Be strong and courageous! Do not be afraid or discouraged. For the LORD your God is with you wherever you go.

JOSHUA 1:9

• • • • • • • • • •

IN MARCH OF 1962, a spring storm sent high winds and huge waves across the low islands of Chincoteague and Assateague off the coasts of Virginia and Maryland. For three days wind, rain, and ocean waves battered the islands, flattening houses and burying cars in sand.

On the Beebe Ranch, water rose higher and higher, threatening to flood Misty's stable. Misty was the Chincoteague pony made famous by Marguerite Henry's book *Misty of Chincoteague* and its movie adaptation. The book tells about the wild ponies of Assateague Island and its annual Pony Penning Day, when ponies are herded across the narrow waterway to Chincoteague Island.

In the book, Paul and Maureen Beebe work to raise money to buy two of those ponies—Phantom and her foal, Misty. Marguerite Henry fictionalized some details, but Phantom, Misty, and the Beebes were all real. But in 1962 Misty was grown up and expecting her own foal in the middle of a terrible storm. Children who had read the book or seen the movie feared for Misty and her coming foal.

When people had to evacuate Chincoteague, they couldn't take animals, but before they left the island, the Beebes moved Misty to the higher ground of their kitchen. The brave little pony stayed there for three days with only a cat for company. The storm left such destruction behind that people couldn't return to Chincoteague for many days. But as soon as they could, the Beebes moved Misty to a veterinarian on the mainland, where she gave birth to a foal they named Stormy. Newspapers carried announcements that Misty and Stormy were safe.

When the storm finally headed out to sea, people came back to find their homes and businesses destroyed. Sadly, over one hundred ponies lost their lives. It would take a lot of money to restore everything, but the movie company agreed to rerelease the Misty movie to help raise the funds. And Misty, with the spindly-legged Stormy clinging to her side, visited theaters and schools. It's not easy for horses to stand calmly as large crowds cheer and clap. But Misty and Stormy bravely faced these events to help the people of Chincoteague recover.

You may never have to face a natural disaster, but hard things sometimes hit us like stormy winds. When that happens, remember that your heavenly Father promises to be with you through the storm and to help you be strong and brave like Misty.

CORRAL YOUR THOUGHTS: Are you or someone you know facing a storm? Write a prayer asking God to be with you or them.

GALLOP INTO ACTION: Write Joshua 1:9 on a card and draw or color a picture of the sun breaking through storm clouds around the verse. Put it in your Bible to remind yourself that God will never leave you, no matter how the dark skies threaten.

FUN NOTES FROM THE BARN: After the storm Marguerite Henry wrote another book about Misty. In *Stormy, Misty's Foal*, the author writes about the storm and thanks the many children who gave their allowances to help the people of Chincoteague recover.

22

ELIJAH

Lost on a Mountain | 1956

Look at the birds. They don't plant or harvest or store food in barns, for your heavenly Father feeds them. And aren't you far more valuable to him than they are?

MATTHEW 6:26

WINTER SNOWS COME EARLY and stay late in the mountains of Colorado. In 1955, when only a few golden leaves still clung to the aspen trees, two horses—a bay and a gray—began climbing higher and higher up a mountain to escape deepening snows. By February, thirty-foot snow drifts (that's like six adults standing on top of each other) had trapped them above the tree line. Not even much grass grows on a 12,800-foot-high ridge, and the two horses were close to starvation. That's when a pilot from a nearby mountain town spotted them as he was flying his small plane in the area.

When the pilot landed back home, he told others about the stranded horses. With snow too deep for a rescue, people decided to air-drop hay to keep them alive until the snow melted. They raised money to buy hay, but by the time the pilot made the first drop, the gray horse was gone and never seen again. The bay horse was still there, though, and the pilot dropped hay to him.

Word spread to a Denver newspaper, and one of its reporters named the horse Elijah, after the Old Testament prophet who was fed by ravens sent by God. Word soon spread even farther, and money and supplies came from all over. Children from around the country sent their allowances to help feed Elijah. A Colorado guide, who led groups of hunters and fishermen into the mountains, thought Elijah might be his packhorse that had strayed back in the fall.

In April, he and others struggled on snowshoes over huge snowdrifts and up the mountain to check on Elijah, who did have the guide's **brand**. The horse was fat and shaggy, but the snow was still too deep to bring Elijah down. Finally, in May the guide was able to shovel a narrow path and lead Elijah down to safety.

People from all over cared for a little packhorse stranded on a mountaintop. God cares even more than that for all his creatures—after all, he created them. Jesus taught that when you see how God takes care of even humble creatures like horses or birds, it can remind you to trust your heavenly Father, who loves you more than those. He'll always faithfully provide for you.

CORRAL YOUR THOUGHTS: Write down three ways God cares for you each day.

GALLOP INTO ACTION: Is there a food bank in your town or church? Ask a parent or caregiver if you can buy a few extra canned goods to share. Your contributions can help those who, like Elijah, are stranded in a time of need.

FUN NOTES FROM THE BARN: A pilot for American Airlines asked for the exact location of Elijah and then, with permission, flew over so passengers could see the hardy horse.

23

SNOWMAN

A Plow Horse Soars as a New Creation | *1958–1962*

If anyone is in Christ, he is a new creation. The old has passed away; behold, the new has come.

2 CORINTHIANS 5:17, ESV

SPOTLIGHTS GLARED DOWN onto the dirt arena, casting confusing shadows around the hurdles. It was so quiet that the crowd at the championship round of the 1958 National Horse Show could hear the thud of Snowman's hooves as he galloped toward the last fence. No other horse had jumped a clear round—not knocking down a rail or bar. If Snowman could clear the last jump, he'd be the national champion and win Horse of the Year.

The audience held its breath as Snowman's rider, Harry de Leyer, crouched forward in the saddle, letting Snowman stretch his neck toward the jump. The gray horse gathered his legs and soared up and over the fence. When Snowman's hooves thumped into the dirt on the other side, the crowd roared. Snowman had captured everyone's heart with his friendliness. Now he had captured the championship.

Just two years before, no one had loved him. He was a dirty, clumsy plow horse. His ribs stuck out, and his hooves were overgrown. Open sores covered his light-gray coat. But Harry saw through the dirt and sores to the horse's heart and took the big horse home to give him a second chance. Harry's children named the horse Snowman and helped him recover. Snowman turned into a gentle giant, carrying young people safely through their first riding lessons.

When Harry sold Snowman to a neighbor, the horse kept jumping fences to come home, so Harry bought him back. He gave the horse more training and helped Snowman become an even stronger jumper. Snowman went from pulling heavy plows to soaring over high jumps.

Do you sometimes feel unloved or misunderstood? Jesus grew up just like you. He was once your age and understands the struggles you face. He sees into your heart and loves you. He died on the cross to give you a whole new life. Just as Snowman gave his heart to Harry and became part of his family, when you give your heart to Jesus, he welcomes you into his family. Through his power, you are a new creation, and with his love and guidance, you will soar to great heights with him.

CORRAL YOUR THOUGHTS: If you've given your heart to Jesus, journal about the ways he loves and guides you. If you haven't done so, you can pray and ask Jesus into your heart. Ask him to forgive your sins and guide you to a new and wonderful life with him.

GALLOP INTO ACTION: Write out 2 Corinthians 5:17 on a card and decorate it with colorful designs. Put it on your wall or tuck it into your Bible to remind yourself that God loves you and that you belong to his family. Then tell a trusted adult so they can pray with you.

FUN NOTES FROM THE BARN: Snowman easily cleared seven-foot-tall jumps, and sometimes Harry even jumped him over another horse.

24

MR. ED

Straight from the Horse's Mouth | *1961–1966*

Some people make cutting remarks, but the words of the wise bring healing.

PROVERBS 12:18

HAVE YOU HEARD OF or watched an old television comedy about a talking horse named Mr. Ed? Between 1961 and 1966, 143 episodes aired, and forty million people tuned in each week to laugh at Ed's antics. In the first episode, Wilbur and Carol Post buy a house in the country and discover a horse in the stable in the backyard. Neighbors tell them the previous owner said whoever bought the house could keep the horse. Carol isn't sure about having a horse, but Wilbur talks her into keeping it.

As Wilbur examines the stable to see if there's room for an office, he begins talking to the horse. Suddenly, to Wilbur's astonishment, the horse talks back. Wilbur rushes to tell everyone, but no one believes him because Mr. Ed will only talk to Wilbur. Carol and the neighbors often hear Wilbur talking with someone, but when they enter the stable, Ed clams up. Ed is also a little mischievous and sometimes says and does things that get Wilbur in trouble. In one episode, Ed enters Wilbur in a contest and wins a miniature horse, but it eats a neighbor's roses and has to go.

Mr. Ed's real name was Bamboo Harvester, and he was a palomino parade horse before his television stardom. To get Ed to move his lips as if he were talking, trainers ran a long nylon fishing line through Ed's mouth and his halter to the trainer off-stage. When the trainer gently pulled on the other end, Ed moved his lips—a natural thing horses do when something moves in their mouths. Eventually, Ed even learned to move his lips on cue while a hidden actor read the lines Ed was supposedly saying. Ed also learned many tricks for the show, using his mouth to pick up phones, hats, pencils, and chess pieces, wave a flag, untie knots, and open and close his stable door.

Mr. Ed's words often got Wilbur in trouble. That was funny in a television show, but if we talked like that with our family and friends, we could cause problems and hurt people we love. In the Bible, Jesus spoke to people with compassion. His words healed and encouraged them. And Jesus sent the

Holy Spirit to help you choose words that encourage and build others up.

CORRAL YOUR THOUGHTS: On the lines below, list some encouraging truths about God's love you can share when friends or family need cheering up.

GALLOP INTO ACTION: Write a letter to someone who needs encouragement. Then share the letter with them.

FUN NOTES FROM THE BARN: Ed learned tricks and worked hard, but sometimes, when he got tired, he'd open his stable door and walk off the set to his corral. He needed a break, and the film crew allowed it.

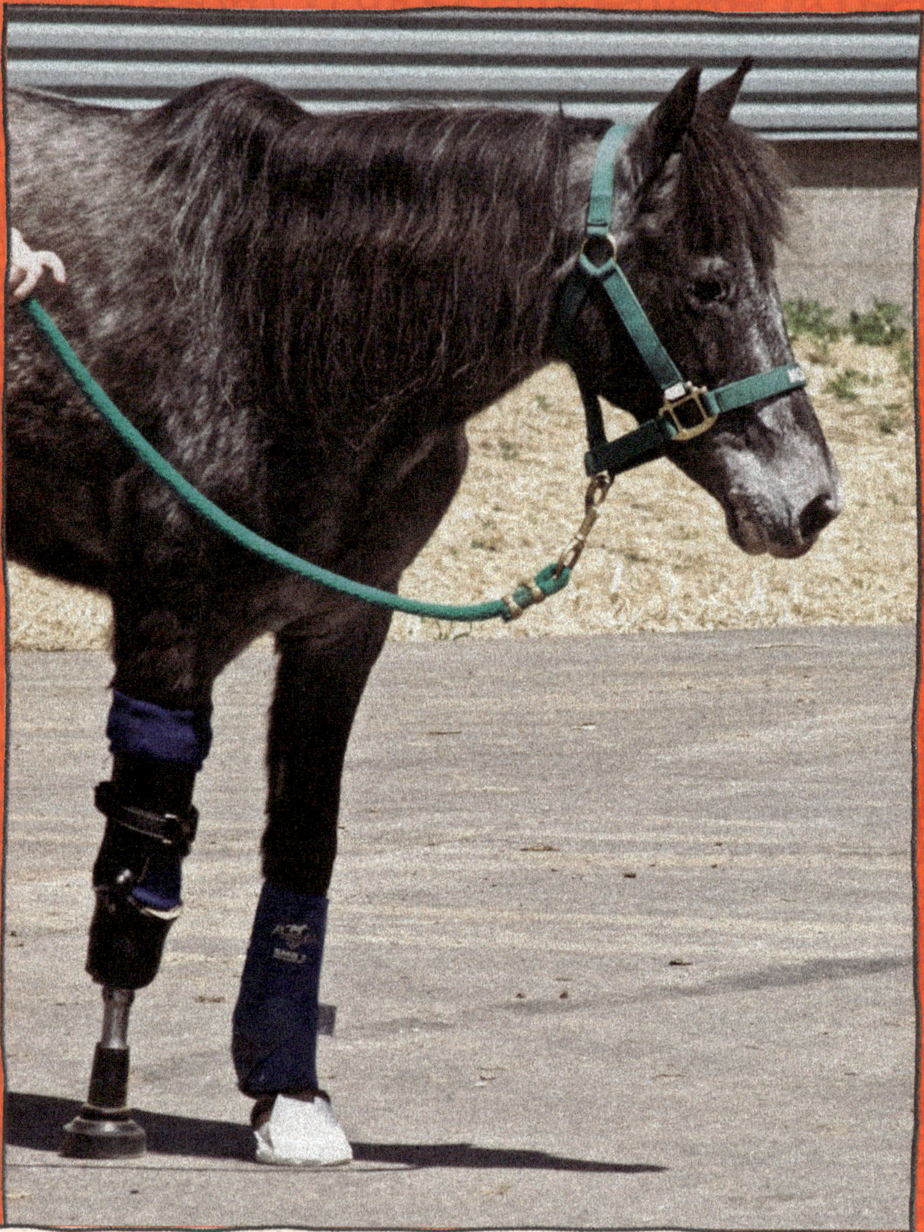

25

MOLLY THE PONY

Survived Two Disasters to Help Others | 2005

[God] comforts us in all our troubles so that we can comfort others.

2 CORINTHIANS 1:4

• • • • • • • • •

IN 2005, HURRICANE KATRINA slammed into the Gulf Coast of the United States, toppling trees and flooding homes, schools, and businesses. Many people evacuated farther inland, but they often had to leave their pets, especially large ones like horses and ponies, behind. Humane societies began rescuing the abandoned animals, but because there were so many, shelters quickly filled up. Ordinary people volunteered to take care of some of the abandoned dogs and cats and horses until their owners could be found.

A lady who kept ponies for children's parties took in some of the abandoned animals, including Molly, a small Pony of the Americas. One day, when Molly and the other ponies were grazing, one of the rescued dogs attacked them. The dog bit Molly's legs and belly and injured her jaw. Molly needed many stitches, and all except one of her wounds healed. The deep wound on Molly's right front leg just wouldn't get better.

It was a hard situation. Amputation, or removal, of a horse's leg is rare, because large animals have trouble getting around on just three legs. Luckily Molly was small, and she was smart—she had already learned to move around and get up and down without putting any weight on her injured leg.

Veterinarians at the Louisiana State University equine clinic amputated Molly's leg below the knee. Molly stayed at the clinic for several weeks so she could heal and so a designer of human artificial limbs could create a leg for her. After a few tries, he came up with one that looked a little like a toilet plunger, but it worked. Molly could even gallop. Molly's owner thought the little pony could help children and adults with disabilities. As they began to visit children with disabilities in hospitals and at camps, Molly knew just what to do. She stood still as she was brushed and patted. Wheelchairs didn't scare her, and she allowed children to touch and inspect her artificial leg. Molly showed them they could live a full life.

Molly was abandoned and then badly injured, but people helped her heal and find a new purpose as a therapy horse for children and adults with disabilities. Have you experienced illness or a disability? Perhaps you've felt a big disappointment or struggled when your family moved a lot. Going through hard times yourself can help you show God's heart of compassion to others going through similar difficulties.

CORRAL YOUR THOUGHTS: How has God helped you through a rough time? Write about it on your journaling lines.

GALLOP INTO ACTION: Do you know someone in your church or school with a long-term illness or disability? Or perhaps someone you know has recently lost a family member. Ask a parent or caregiver for ideas on how you can befriend and support them.

FUN NOTES FROM THE BARN: Because so many animals died in Hurricane Katrina or never found their owners afterward, the United States now requires natural disaster evacuation plans to include companion animals.

26

BREEZE

Abandoned at Birth | 2013

I am leaving you with a gift—peace of mind and heart. And the peace I give is a gift the world cannot give. So don't be troubled or afraid.

JOHN 14:27

WHEN YOU WERE LITTLE, did you have a teddy bear or other plush animal you hugged and snuggled with when you went to bed? Breeze, an abandoned Dartmoor pony foal, loved to cuddle with his teddy bear too. Only Breeze's teddy was four feet tall and encircled him like a hug when he pressed into its soft fur.

Many Dartmoor ponies, one of Britain's native pony breeds, still roam the high moors, or hills, of Dartmoor National Park in southwestern England. These small, hardy ponies survive in a windy area of coarse grass and heather. In the past, Dartmoor ponies were sometimes used in mines or as pack ponies. Today, local farmers keep Dartmoor ponies for driving or as children's ponies. In fact, it was a local farmer who alerted a mare and foal sanctuary in the area about a newborn pony that seemed to be abandoned.

When rescuers arrived, the days-old foal had collapsed from cold and lack of milk. They couldn't find his mother, so they took the foal to the sanctuary. Even though they didn't know if he'd live, they named him Breeze. A veterinarian began treatment right away, giving the foal fluids and medicines and mare's milk. The sanctuary staff pitched in with around-the-clock feedings and care. But just like human babies, foals also need to feel loved and safe, so the sanctuary sent out a request for large plush animals. People in the area gave all kinds of these, including a four-foot-tall teddy bear. The staff named the bear Buttons and put the giant teddy in Breeze's stall. The lonely little foal loved Buttons, nuzzling and nestling into it for reassurance when he was afraid.

Breeze had a hard start to his life, but he found peace with Buttons. No matter what age we are, scary things can happen. Bad storms, moving to a new city, illnesses, your family going through divorce, a military parent getting deployed on dangerous assignments—all these can make you feel lost and anxious, but God gives the gift of peace.

When Jesus was arrested, his friends ran away, leaving him alone. So he understands when you are troubled and fearful, and he promises he'll never leave you. When you're feeling scared or anxious, you can always snuggle into his comforting arms.

CORRAL YOUR THOUGHTS: Write about a time when you felt afraid but Jesus gave you peace.

GALLOP INTO ACTION: Do you have younger siblings who sometimes get scared? Or a friend going through a hard time? You can be God's arms and give them a giant teddy bear hug.

FUN NOTES FROM THE BARN: The sanctuary staff gave Breeze colostrum right away. It's a super nutritious milk that mammal mothers produce for their babies in their first few days of life. It protects the foals from diseases too.

PART 3

God Made Horses Special

HORSES ARE PREY ANIMALS. You can tell because their eyes are on the sides of their heads so they can quickly spot sneaky predators like wolves. But that's just one of the special features God gave horses. He gave them springy legs to run with the wind and swiveling ears to hear your softest whisper. In this section you'll learn about the superpowers that make horses such great companions and helpers for people.

27

HERD ANIMALS

Horses Love Company

A friend loves at all times.

PROVERBS 17:17, ESV

HORSES ARE HERD ANIMALS, and they love company. Foals form their first close bonds with their mothers. When they're a little older, young horses enjoy racing each other and rearing up to play fight. They may kick out their long legs or buck just for the fun of it. Calmer, older horses graze in small groups of two or three friends. During hot afternoons horses like to stand head to tail with their best buddies, tails swishing flies away from each other.

Not all horses get to live with other horses, though. Racehorses often travel a lot and can become nervous and hard to handle without friends. A famous racehorse named Seabiscuit was like that, so his trainer provided animal friends for him. A calm cow horse named Pumpkin, a stray dog named Pocatell, and a spider monkey named Jo Jo all traveled everywhere with Seabiscuit.

Family horses may also live alone, because another horse would be too expensive to feed or too big for the family's space. So, like Seabiscuit's trainer, the family may get the horse a barn buddy such as a dog or goat. Goats are small and even eat the weeds that horses turn up their noses at. Donkeys and miniature horses also make good buddies. They eat what horses eat but are cheaper to feed and house. Donkeys even make good guard animals—it's hard to ignore a braying donkey when it senses danger. Each horse is unique, though, and some have befriended cats and even pigs and chickens.

Whether it's another horse, a goat, or a donkey, horses love spending time with friends, and so do we. Friends often sit together at lunch. Friends are loyal. They listen to each other and keep each other company when one of them is worried. And friends don't have to be exactly alike. Be like a horse and don't be afraid to befriend someone with different interests or from a different cultural background than you. Even if you like different activities or your families have different customs, you can still be buddies, and you'll help each other grow into more loving and considerate friends.

Whether your friend is just like you or a little different, arguments sometimes happen. God understands that and encourages you to love your friend at all times, especially when you disagree. A loving friend takes time to discuss the problem and isn't afraid to apologize.

CORRAL YOUR THOUGHTS: Think about what makes a good friend. Write about some ways you can support your "herd."

GALLOP INTO ACTION: This week, do something special for a friend to let them know you care.

FUN NOTES FROM THE BARN: In a herd of wild horses, an older mare leads the group to food and water and safe places to rest, while the stallion is the herd's protector.

28

360-DEGREE VISION

Seeing All Around

Ever since the world was created, people have seen the earth and sky. Through everything God made, they can clearly see his invisible qualities—his eternal power and divine nature.

ROMANS 1:20

HAS A FRIEND EVER sneaked up on you and made you jump? You may have screamed, and your heart probably beat faster for a few seconds, but you were soon okay. However, if a predator like a wolf was able to sneak up and surprise a horse, the horse could lose its life. To protect horses, God gave their eyes fantastic features that help them spot sneaky predators, at night or during the day.

Horses have some of the biggest eyes of any land mammal. At night, when many predators prowl, a horse's large pupils expand, letting in more light. Another structure, the tapetum lucidum, reflects the light coming into their eyes like a mirror, intensifying the light. It's also what makes the eyes of horses and cats and some other animals glow in the dark. With more light coming in and lots of rod-shaped eye cells designed to work in low light, horses see better at night than humans.

But dangers exist in daylight, too, so God put a horse's eyes high up on the sides of their heads. When horses put their heads down to graze, they can still scan all around for predators. They don't even have to turn their heads because each eye has a different view of the surroundings. That allows horses to see almost 360 degrees around.

Bright sunlight can make it hard to see. People sometimes wear hats with visors to shade their eyes, but horses don't need hats. A dark, bumpy structure hangs out a little over the horse's iris (the colored part of the eye). This, together with their thick, downward-slanting eyelashes, creates a natural sun visor.

Horses always need to watch for danger, and their eyes are made to scan for movement all around. But horses don't see details or colors as well as you do. God designed your eyes to see both far away *and* up close. You can see stars twinkling high in the night sky, and you can focus on the beauty of a butterfly wing. God wants us to see that all creation proclaims the work of his hands and to come to believe in him.

CORRAL YOUR THOUGHTS: Do you take time to notice the beauty of creation each day? Write about something beautiful you noticed today.

GALLOP INTO ACTION: Write a poem thanking God for his beautiful world and share it with a friend.

FUN NOTES FROM THE BARN: When wind blows dust into a horse's eyes, they have a built-in system that removes it. A third eyelid (called the nictitating membrane) moves fast across their eyes to wipe away the dust. It even releases tears to help wash out the dust, acting like the windshield wipers of a car.

29

ALL EARS

Listening Up

Tune your ears to wisdom, and concentrate on understanding. . . . Then you will understand what is right, just, and fair, and you will find the right way to go.

PROVERBS 2:2,9

CAN YOU WIGGLE YOUR EARS? Only about 10 to 20 percent of people can. Scientists have discovered that when we humans hear something we're interested in, we can make very slight ear movements toward the sound. But horses can top that—they can swivel each ear 180 degrees around.

Each of a horse's ears has ten muscles used for movement, compared to our three. So when a horse hears a stall door banging or dogs barking, it can turn one or both of its funnel-like ears toward the sound. Horses are prey animals and must use every sense to keep a lookout for predators. Being able to point their ears toward a sound helps horses decide if it means danger. Horses also have excellent hearing. They can hear you whisper. And their ears can pick up sounds from 2.5 miles away. No wonder a faraway car horn that we don't even hear can startle a horse.

Pitch, or frequency (how high or low a sound is), is another important factor in what horses can hear. Sounds travel through the air in waves. Rapidly vibrating waves produce high-pitched sounds like a baby's cry or a dog whistle's screech. People can't hear a dog whistle, but horses can. The low rumble of distant thunder comes from slowly vibrating sound waves. Horses can hear an approaching thunderstorm way before us.

Because horses have great hearing, windy days often make them restless. The wind may carry distant sounds, like the crash of a trash can blowing over, from farther away than usual. Branches and leaves rattling in the wind may muffle close-up sounds. On those days, horses can become confused about which sounds are important to listen to.

Like a noisy wind, electronic devices send us messages from near and far, sometimes confusing or muffling God's Word. How can we know what to listen to? Proverbs tells us to turn our ears to the wisdom that comes from God through his Word. We can do that best when we turn off the distractions.

Then we can hear God, and our hearts will understand what is right and just and fair.

CORRAL YOUR THOUGHTS: On the lines below, keep track of how much time you spend on electronic devices for two or three days. Talk with a parent or caregiver about whether you're spending too much time on them.

GALLOP INTO ACTION: Decide to have a quiet time each day when you shut off your phone or other electronic devices and turn your ears to God's Word. It doesn't have to be a long time.

FUN NOTES FROM THE BARN: Horses can learn many voice commands when people use them consistently. The pitch the rider uses also gives them clues. For example, using a low voice for "whoa" and a higher voice for "walk on" helps horses understand humans.

30

HORSE TALK

Communication in the Barn

O my people, trust in him at all times. Pour out your hearts to him, for God is our refuge.

PSALM 62:8

EVEN BEFORE A FOAL stands on its gangly legs, its mother sniffs and licks it all over. She **nickers** softly, encouraging her foal to get up. This is a bonding time for the mare and her foal to learn each other's scent and sounds. The foal must always recognize its mother and trot close beside her for safety and nourishment.

Horses communicate well with sounds. Besides the soft nickers of a mare to her foal, horses **whinny** to keep in touch with other horses in nearby pastures or to let them know something's happening. Horses snort sharply if they suspect danger or need to clear dust out of their noses, but they blow softly to say hello. Horses may nicker to welcome you when you enter the barn, especially if it's feeding time.

A horse's body language expresses even more

than its sounds do. A relaxed horse stands with its head lowered and the tip of one hind hoof resting on the ground. A friendly horse faces people or other horses and may slowly stretch its head and neck forward if it's curious. But when a horse hears something it doesn't recognize, it will raise its head and point its ears toward the sound.

With their sounds and body language, horses show that they feel emotions just as we do. A mare and her foal care deeply for each other, and when separated from its mother, the foal feels scared. Horses have special friends just like you, and if one leaves, they feel sad and lonely. Big storms can scare them, and when they're in pain or confused, horses get worried or even angry.

Sometimes when sadness, anger, loneliness, or worry overwhelms you, it can be hard to express your feelings in words. But Jesus understands you, whether you use words or not. He grew up just like you and lived through scary storms and had loved ones who got sick. He understands your quiet tears as well as your huff and puff of anger, so you can pour out your heart to him.

Jesus promises that you can trust him to know your struggle and to be your refuge. Like a mare who cares for and protects her foal, he will keep you close and safe.

CORRAL YOUR THOUGHTS: Write about a time when you felt scared or sad or angry.

GALLOP INTO ACTION: Left untended, emotions can grow like weeds in a pasture. So when you're sad or angry, pour out your feelings to Jesus. Ask him to hold you close as you trot beside him each day. You can also talk to a trusted adult about your emotions.

FUN NOTES FROM THE BARN: To understand horses, watch their ears. Dozing horses may let their ears droop. Horses may put one ear back to pay attention to their rider, but stiff, pinned-back ears can show anger or fear.

31

HORSE TEETH

Made to Last

You must grow in the grace and knowledge of our Lord and Savior Jesus Christ.

2 PETER 3:18

DO YOU REMEMBER WAY BACK to when you had a loose baby tooth? Did you like to wiggle it with your tongue until you could finally pull it out? Foals have baby teeth too—called milk teeth—which fall out naturally when they stop nursing and begin to graze. Just like your baby teeth, a foal's milk teeth are gradually replaced with adult teeth. By around five years of age, horses have all their adult teeth. Mares usually have thirty-six, and males have forty.

Once you have your adult, or permanent, teeth, your parents and dentist will probably tell you to brush often so your adult teeth will last all your life. No one needs to tell horses that, because their adult teeth usually do last almost as long as they live. Horses have strong, sharp cutting teeth, called incisors, in the front of their mouths. They need these to rip up bunches of grass and weeds. But two-thirds of their teeth are molars, wide back teeth that grind up all the tough stems of hay and grass.

Even with so many molars, the daily grinding would wear a horse's teeth down flat in just a few years. So underneath each of their adult teeth, the Lord gave them several more inches of tooth called the reserve crown. Over the years, as the tooth above the gum wears down, more and more of those spare inches of tooth gradually erupt, or push up, through the gum. Not until a horse is over twenty-five will the reserve crown be mostly used up.

When foals start grazing on grass, their milk teeth fall out because they need grown-up teeth to be able to chew and digest the food that will help them grow up physically strong. As believers, we need to grow up strong spiritually. When we chew and digest the good food of the Scriptures, we grow in the grace and knowledge of the Lord Jesus, our Savior.

CORRAL YOUR THOUGHTS: Journal about some actions you can take to grow strong spiritually, such as reading your Bible daily or memorizing Scripture.

GALLOP INTO ACTION: Pray and ask God to help you put one of those actions into practice this week.

FUN NOTES FROM THE BARN: Horses need regular dental exams just like people. Among other problems, they sometimes develop sharp points on their teeth that can cause sores on their cheeks and tongues. A vet or dentist for horses can file down those points so the horse's teeth wear more evenly in a procedure called floating.

32

THE INTERDENTAL SPACE

Perfect for the Bit

I will guide you along the best pathway for your life. I will advise you and watch over you. Do not be like a senseless horse or mule that needs a bit and bridle to keep it under control.

PSALM 32:8-9

DO YOU ENJOY BITING into a crisp apple? Horses love apples too. If you give them an apple, they use their front cutting teeth, called incisors, to bite off sweet, juicy chunks. Then their molars crunch those big bites into small bits they can swallow. You also have incisors and molars, and you use them in the same way. But horses have much larger incisors and molars. They can tear off great clumps of grass or hay and then grind them up like veggies in a blender.

Horses also have longer heads than you, which means they have something you don't have—a wide gap, known as the interdental space, between their incisors and molars. Only gum tissue covers the section of the jawbone that forms the side of this gap, called the **bars**. It's like the space left whenever you lose a baby tooth, only larger and permanent. The bars are super sensitive to pressure.

Ancient people discovered that the interdental gap was perfect for a wood, bone, or metal **bit**, which would improve communication with their horses. Straps on the **bridle** hold the bit in place, and the **reins** also attach to the bit. The rider uses the reins to apply pressure to the sensitive bars, helping the horse understand the rider's commands.

Today, most bits are metal or rubber-coated metal and come in two major types—**snaffle** and **curb bits**. Within these two categories, there are many styles, sizes, and combinations of bits. So it's important to find the kind that works best for each horse—one that doesn't cause pain but helps the horse pay attention.

God has given you something even more sensitive than the bars in a horse's mouth—your heart. When you read God's Word regularly, your heart becomes more open to understanding God's wise guidance. Think about it. The Creator who made the world and all its amazing animals, including horses, loves you. And he wants to guide you along the paths that are just right for you and your interests and talents.

CORRAL YOUR THOUGHTS: On the lines below, list the ways God's Word guides you.

GALLOP INTO ACTION: Find a little time each day to read a psalm or chapter in your Bible. If you have an assignment book, write the time down and ask God to help you keep that time just for him. Don't worry if you miss a time occasionally. God will always be right there ready to talk with you.

FUN NOTES FROM THE BARN: When Native Americans began taming and riding horses, they made bits out of twisted buffalo hair or horsehair. They looped these rope bits through the horse's interdental space and around its jaws. Then they grabbed the long end of that rope and leaped on for a dash across the plains.

33

SPEEDY DIGESTION

Eat and Run

**Our Father in heaven. . . .
Give us today the food
we need.**

MATTHEW 6:9, 11

IF YOU'VE EVER GOTTEN pieces of hay down the back of your shirt, you know how stiff and scratchy it can be. That's because of cellulose, a tough fiber that helps the plant keep its shape. People can't digest cellulose, but herbivores—animals that only eat grasses and plants—can digest it. Some herbivores, like cows, will graze for a while then lie down and regurgitate, or bring up, what they ate to rechew it and further break up the cellulose. But God designed horses to be able to eat and run.

In their natural habitat, horses stay on the move, grazing as they go, for twelve to sixteen hours a day. During the day they may gradually eat up to thirty pounds of different kinds of plants. Many of those plants are coarse grasses with lots of cellulose, but horses don't have time to lie down and rechew all that rough food. Wild horses always need to be ready to flee danger, even if they're in the middle of a great meal.

Horses can't burp or vomit either, so what goes down has to go all the way through the digestive system. If all that rough stuff gets stuck inside, the horse can become very sick. So God gave horses an organ in their digestive system called the **cecum** to help them digest the plants they eat. In the cecum, good bacteria break down cellulose into smaller molecules that the horse can use. Because of this process, horses can get more nutrition and energy from weeds and other tough plants than many herbivores can. And in the winter, the digestive process occurring in the cecum produces heat that helps keep horses warm.

A horse's cecum keeps working even when the horse is eating and running. Sometimes your days are so busy with school and other activities that you may have to eat and run too. That can make it hard to remember to thank God for your family and home, food and clothing, school and friends—and all the many blessings he gives you each day.

In Matthew 6:8, Jesus promises that your heavenly Father knows your needs even before you ask. He then shares a very special prayer called the

Lord's Prayer. We can pray this prayer to thank God for giving us food and so many more blessings each day.

CORRAL YOUR THOUGHTS: Do you remember to thank God for his daily blessings? Write a prayer to thank him in your journaling space.

GALLOP INTO ACTION: Each day, be on the lookout for blessings from God and make it a point to thank him before you go to sleep.

FUN NOTES FROM THE BARN: Horses have twenty-five thousand taste buds compared to the roughly eight thousand that people have. This, along with their keen sense of smell, helps horses avoid poisonous plants and unhealthy water but also means that their owners often have to hide medicines in applesauce or frosting.

34

HORSE COLORS AND MARKINGS

Snips, Stars, and Stockings

There is no longer Jew or Greek, slave or free, male and female. For you are all one in Christ Jesus.

GALATIANS 3:28

HOW DO YOU TELL a bay horse from a chestnut horse? What's the difference between a snip and a star on a horse's face? Or socks and stockings on a horse's legs? You can read whole books about horse colors and markings, so let's look at just a few of the more common ones.

Bays and chestnuts can be found in many breeds, and they are two of the most common horse colors. Because there are many shades of browns for bay horses and reds for chestnut horses, a dark chestnut horse could be mistaken for a reddish bay. You might easily confuse the colors unless you look at the horses' manes, tails, ears, and legs. Bay horses have black manes and tails and black on the edges of their ears and on their legs. Chestnut horses have manes and tails that are the same color as their coats or lighter, and they have no black on their legs or ears.

Coat colors can change with age or between winter and summer, but white markings on horses' heads and legs remain the same throughout their lives. Markings can be in combination with almost any coat color. A narrow band of white just above a horse's hoof is called a **coronet**. White that reaches a little farther up is a **sock**, and if it reaches to the knees (on the front legs) or the **hocks** (a joint on the hind legs), it's a **stocking**.

Stars and **blazes** are common on horses' faces. A star is a roundish shape between a horse's eyes, while a snip is a small white shape on the nose. Blazes go from above the eyes down to the horse's **muzzle** and can be narrow or wide. If the white hair covers almost all the face, the horse has a **bald face**—even though there's lots of hair.

All domestic and wild horses and ponies, no matter their color, are members of the *Equus caballus* species. In the human family there's also a great variety of skin and eye and hair color, but we are all human beings, of the species *Homo sapiens*. Sometimes we may feel hesitant about getting to know people who look a little different than us, but remember that we are all made in the image of our heavenly Father, worthy of being loved and known. And when we become part of God's family, no matter the color of our hair or eyes or skin, we are all dressed in one type of clothing, the righteousness of Christ. We are all part of his herd.

CORRAL YOUR THOUGHTS: In the journaling space, list some things that might make someone your age feel different and perhaps get left out.

GALLOP INTO ACTION: If you know someone like that, pray for them and ask God to show you ways to reach out and befriend them.

FUN NOTES FROM THE BARN: Did you know that Friesian horses are always black? Or that many Akhal-Teke horses have a metallic sheen to their coats?

35

SLEEPING UPRIGHT

Standing Firm

God is faithful; he will not allow the temptation to be more than you can stand. When you are tempted, he will show you a way out so that you can endure.

1 CORINTHIANS 10:13

IT'S A WARM AFTERNOON in your classroom. You feel sleepy and prop your head on your arm as you listen to the teacher. Before you know it, you're doing a nosedive toward your desk. Just before your head smacks down, your eyes snap open, and you jerk your head up. You blink and look around, hoping no one noticed. When you fell asleep, your arm went floppy like the spaghetti noodles you had for lunch.

This never happens to horses, because when horses need a short snooze, they can sleep standing up. They may not always feel safe enough to lie down, and if they had to gather their long legs together to scramble up, they could lose their lives to a stealthy predator. So God gave them a special way to survive in the wild when they need to quickly gallop away, leaving predators in the dust.

A combination of tendons and ligaments called the stay apparatus stabilizes, or holds steady, the joints of the front legs and the lower joints of the back legs. The back legs also have a reciprocal apparatus between their stifles and their hocks, which are similar to your knees and ankles. When a horse puts its weight on one leg, this apparatus locks the stifle and hock in position. The horse can even rest one hind leg at a time, switching back and forth every few minutes. When a horse dozes, its breathing and heart rate slow and its neck and head may hang down, but it will never do a nosedive.

Like a horse, you may sometimes face tough situations. If you forget to study, you may be tempted to cheat on a test. Or you may want to join in gossip about a classmate. God gave horses a way to stand firm to escape trouble, and God has given you a way to stand firm against troubling temptations too.

You don't need to spend time gathering special words. In the twitch of a pony's ear, you can pray to your heavenly Father, and he'll listen and help you defeat temptations. He may encourage you to stand strong against cheating and to remember to study next time. Or he may encourage you to gallop away and leave gossipers in the dust.

CORRAL YOUR THOUGHTS: Have you ever been tempted to do something wrong? Ask God to show you ways to stand firm against temptations and write down your thoughts.

GALLOP INTO ACTION: Share your plan with a friend or trusted adult and ask them to pray for you. Having a plan and prayer partners will help you resist temptations.

FUN NOTES FROM THE BARN: Horses and ponies don't need as much deep sleep as humans. Horses stand and snooze for many short naps each day and only need to lie down for deep sleep for two to three hours a day.

36

TOP-SPEED LEGS

A Spring in Their Step

Those who trust in the LORD will find new strength. They will soar high on wings like eagles. They will run and not grow weary.

ISAIAH 40:31

DO YOU REMEMBER TIGGER, the orange-and-black-striped tiger who is a friend of Winnie-the-Pooh? In the stories, Tigger uses his tail like a spring. As he bounces on his tail, it squeezes down and then releases to launch Tigger into the air. He bounces from tree to rock and, to Pooh's dismay, often onto Pooh.

In real life, scientists have found that a few small creatures have springs a little like Tigger's in their legs. One of these, the grasshopper, can bounce high off the sidewalk when you get too close. But the biggest animal with springs in its legs is the horse. The springs in horses' legs don't make them bouncy. Instead, they help horses gallop tirelessly until they win a race or escape a predator.

To efficiently cover ground in a gallop, a horse

must stretch out each leg and then contract it, or pull it back, fast for the next stride. Muscles alone would do that slowly and tire quickly. But God designed the muscles and tendons in a horse's legs to work together to *gather* energy when the leg comes back—like a coiled spring. That coiled spring then releases and catapults the leg forward for the next stride. This spring works so fast that it took modern photography to prove that all four legs are off the ground in one stride of a horse's gallop. A horse's speedy forty-three miles per hour makes it one of the top ten fastest mammals on earth.

You may not often run in races, but each day you probably have schoolwork and maybe some chores to do. Sometimes you may get tired of your work and feel like quitting—not a good thing for your grades or helping your family. God didn't give you springs to keep going, but he's given you something even better—his promise that when you hope in him, he'll give you the strength you need to gallop to the finish line of your work.

CORRAL YOUR THOUGHTS: On the journaling lines, list three things that might help you gather energy to keep going to finish your schoolwork or chores.

GALLOP INTO ACTION: This week try one or two of your journal ideas to see if they help you complete your work.

FUN NOTES FROM THE BARN: When horses are born, their legs are already 90 percent of the length of adult horse legs. They may have a little trouble getting up at first, but within just one day, foals can buck and gallop alongside their mothers.

37

HORSE FEATHERS

A Fluffy Protection

He will cover you with his feathers. He will shelter you with his wings. His faithful promises are your armor and protection.

PSALM 91:4

PINK FLAMINGO FEATHERS. Sleek, black penguin feathers. Glittery hummingbird feathers. Birds have feathers to show off to their mates, to keep warm, and mostly, to fly. But horses? Do they really have feathers? And if so, what good are they?

First of all, horses don't really have feathers. It's just one of the many funny names people have for some parts of a horse. Feathers, also called feathering, are long, thick hairs that grow down from the lower part of some horses' legs. Many horses have some longer hair growing on the back of their legs, but that isn't feathering. Feathering covers the lower legs and hooves, front and back, like a feather duster.

Secondly, feathers are found mostly on draft horses and ponies—those that were once used for farmwork or hauling wagons. Lots of draft horse breeds, such as Clydesdales, Friesians, and Shires, were native to colder places where roads and fields were often muddy and covered in brambles and rocks. For these large workhorses, feathering protected their legs like thick leggings or pants. Small rocks bounced off feathering, and thorns couldn't pierce it. Feathers kept horses' legs warm and dry when they pulled wagons or plows through cold, sticky mud. Best of all, feathering helped water and mud slide right off a draft horse's legs.

Sometimes when people say mean things about you behind your back or online, you may feel like they're throwing rocks at you or bogging you down with their muddy lies. Like thorns, their unkind words can pierce right through you. Jesus experienced people who wanted to throw rocks at him, and many spread lies about him too. In the end, they even pierced him with a crown of thorns. So he understands how you feel and promises that when you're hurt, he'll cover you with his wings, the way a bird covers its young. He will shield you with his strong feathers so the mud and rocks and thorns slide right off.

CORRAL YOUR THOUGHTS: In the Bible, when King David was stuck in the muddy lies spread by others, he poured out his pain to God in the Psalms and asked for God's help. Write a psalm of your own, telling God about a time when someone's words hurt you.

GALLOP INTO ACTION: One way God helps us is by providing people to talk to. When someone is saying unkind things or spreading lies about you, talk to a trusted adult who can help you know the best action to take.

FUN NOTES FROM THE BARN: Some breeds of horses have such thick feathering that you can hardly see their hooves until they trot. Then their fluffy feathers whirl, making it look like they're dancing.

38

CUSHIONING THE BLOW

A Frog in Each Hoof

Let your unfailing love comfort me.

PSALM 119:76

IF YOU PICKED UP a horse's hoof and a frog croaked or leaped out at you, you'd probably leap back with a croak of your own. Of course, that's not going to happen, but there is an important structure on the bottom of each hoof that we *call* a frog. Some think it's because its rubbery shape looks a little like the back of a sitting frog. Wherever the term came from, farriers—equine specialists who care for and shoe horses' hooves—as well as veterinarians tell us how important the frog is for cushioning the hoof and for blood circulation.

Horses are large, heavy animals, so their hooves must absorb many shocks. When they gallop, jump, or turn quickly, horses often land on just one hoof at a time. That's a lot of weight on one hoof, but the frog helps cushion the blow. When each hoof is off the ground, blood vessels in its frog fill with blood. When the hoof lands, the blood vessels in the frog spread out—a little like a squishy sponge—and absorb a lot of the impact.

Another important thing happens when each hoof hits the ground. The impact pushes the blood in the frog back up the horse's legs to the horse's heart. From there the heart pumps the blood on its new journey to remove waste products and pick up more oxygen and nutrients.

If horses didn't have frogs in their hooves to cushion their legs when they land on hard ground, the impact could crush their leg bones. Sometimes a bad grade, an unkind comment, or not making a team can feel like a crushing blow to us, but God can cushion the impact.

Jesus suffered many hard blows before he was crucified, and on the cross he was crushed for our sins. When you land in hard situations at school or in your family, remember that Jesus understands how it feels. You can trust him to be there to comfort you, tenderly cushioning and protecting your heart so the impact doesn't harm you.

CORRAL YOUR THOUGHTS: Write about a time when Jesus' love comforted and protected your heart when it felt crushed.

GALLOP INTO ACTION: Do you have a friend or family member whose heart is hurting or breaking? Pray for them and write an encouraging note to tell them that you and Jesus love them.

FUN NOTES FROM THE BARN: Would you believe that each of a horse's hooves is just one toe? Only animals in the Equidae family, such as horses, ponies, donkeys, and zebras, walk on one-toed hooves. A horse's toes are strong enough to bear over two times the horse's weight when it takes off in a gallop, yet light enough to make sudden turns.

PART 4

Activities with Horses

MOST HORSE SPORTS AND ACTIVITIES grew out of work that horses once did. English-style dressage and eventing came from military and hunting traditions in Europe. Western-style events came from skills that were needed on ranches to care for livestock. No matter which activity you enjoy, the many abilities of horses make them ideal partners.

Like other sports, activities with horses require the right equipment. In the horse world, tack—short for *tackle*—describes all the equipment needed to care for and ride horses. "Tacking up" means getting a horse ready for a ride. In this section, you'll learn about equestrian sports and activities, as well as tack and equipment that make riding safe and comfortable for both horse and rider.

39

BARREL RACING

Win the Prize

All athletes are disciplined in their training. They do it to win a prize that will fade away, but we do it for an eternal prize.

1 CORINTHIANS 9:25

BARREL RACING IS A popular rodeo event. Racing against the clock, riders gallop their horses in a cloverleaf pattern around three large barrels arranged in a triangle. To begin, the horse and rider team catapults into the arena and gallops to their first barrel. They hug the barrel in a tight, fast turn that sprays dirt in all directions. Coming out of the circle, they straighten and dash to the next barrel. When they've circled all three barrels, they sprint as fast as they can out of the arena.

To win, a team just needs a faster time than anyone else. Sound easy? Not so fast. To be a successful barrel racer, a horse must be in top shape and have speed and agility. So it takes lots of training before a horse and rider team even enters an arena for a show. Riders walk and trot their horses over long distances to build cardiovascular strength. (That's the ability of the horse's heart and lungs to send oxygen to its muscles.) To improve agility for those tight turns, riders trot their horses over ground poles and do many large and small circles. In practice sessions, riders may also ask their horses to lengthen and shorten their strides within a gait, which builds muscle strength.

When riders decide to become barrel racers, they want to win, and they train hard for prizes like fancy belt buckles, new saddles, and even big money at the upper levels. But buckles tarnish, saddles wear out, and money gets spent.

When you trust in Jesus, he begins to transform your heart so that you want to please him with your words and actions. But that's not always easy, so Jesus has given you the Holy Spirit to train you for the challenges in this race called life. He gives you stamina to persevere when the going gets hard. He gives you power to defeat temptations from the evil one. He helps you be strong and agile when unexpected things happen.

And when he's helped you run your race, you'll receive the prize of eternal life with him—a prize that won't tarnish or fade away.

CORRAL YOUR THOUGHTS: How is the Holy Spirit transforming you to be more like Jesus? Write about it on your journaling lines.

GALLOP INTO ACTION: When you have worked hard and done well on a test, in a game, or in a chore at home, thank God for helping you do well and glorify him with your work.

FUN NOTES FROM THE BARN: You don't want to lose your hat in a barrel race! Some contestants poke long bobby pins through their hair and hat-band. Others stick double-sided tape on their fore-heads, and some use both methods.

40

DRILL TEAMS AND QUADRILLES

All Together Now

As each has received a gift, use it to serve one another.

1 PETER 4:10, ESV

CAVALRY UNITS—GROUPS OF mounted soldiers—were important in wars before motorized vehicles came along. Sometimes they scouted ahead, but often they rode in unison to charge through an enemy's defenses. Battle lines of horses galloped forward **stirrup** to stirrup or moved sideways to meet approaching armies. Military schools trained riders and horses in those movements and sometimes put on exhibitions for royalty and visiting diplomats.

Today, we see some of these same movements in Western **drill teams**. Lines of riders in Western clothing gallop their horses into and around an arena, flags flying. They create star and wheel patterns for cheering audiences.

In France, in addition to the cavalry schools, another group riding activity became popular in the 1700s. Horse and rider groups of four performed patterns to specially written music. These were often called horse ballets, and the groups were called **quadrilles** after a French dance of the same name.

Quadrilles are sometimes performed at present-day dressage shows. Four, or a multiple of four, riders in helmets and tall black boots trot their horses in a line into a dressage arena. After fanning out to stop and salute the judge, the quadrille team walks, trots, and canters in precise figures to music.

Whichever activity you prefer, riding on a team is fun and good for both horses and riders. Everyone must work patiently and use their unique skills for the team. Faster horses usually work better on the outside of a pattern. Slower horses may be more patient and get along better on the inside. A rider who's good at memorizing the figures may make a good leader. Those that follow must be skilled at keeping the uniform spaces needed to ride drills.

We often have to work in groups in our schools and families to get projects like science experiments or yard work done. Just like on a drill team, each member needs to use their special skills to help the group. For school projects, one person may do the measurements while another member creates a poster. At home, younger children might rake, and an older child can load up the wheelbarrow.

Working with others is not always easy, but when you pray and ask the Holy Spirit for patience with others, you'll find the best way for you to serve in your group.

CORRAL YOUR THOUGHTS: What do you like or not like about working in groups? Write about it below.

GALLOP INTO ACTION: List some skills God has given you that would be helpful to a group.

FUN NOTES FROM THE BARN: Riders on teams must keep an even spacing between the horses in front of and behind them when they're in a line. When they perform movements with a horse across from them, they need to be in line with that horse and begin and end their movements at the same time.

41

EVENTING

Trust Your Navigator

Do not be afraid or discouraged, for the LORD will personally go ahead of you. He will be with you; he will neither fail you nor abandon you.

DEUTERONOMY 31:8

WOULD YOU JUMP OVER an obstacle if you couldn't see what was on the other side? Eventing horses do it all the time. Eventing, or combined training competitions, have three phases—dressage, cross-country jumping, and show jumping. Horses compete in all three phases, but the cross-country course may challenge horses to trust their navigators or riders the most.

Horses' eyes are on the sides of their heads. That's great for spotting sneaky predators, but it means horses have a narrower range of what's called binocular vision than humans do. Binocular vision is when two eyes work together to create a three-dimensional view. Because humans have good binocular vision, they have better depth perception (knowing how far away or close an object is) than horses do.

Having eyes on the side of their heads also

creates blind spots for horses—right behind them, and, more important for jumping, right in front of their faces and under their noses. There's a third vision challenge horses have: Their eyes take longer than ours to adjust when they go from light to dark places.

Cross-country courses go through woods and fields and up and down hills. They have twenty-four to thirty-six natural looking obstacles. Sometimes there's a jump just as the horse and rider are about to enter a dark wood. The horse's eyes can't adjust quickly, so it must jump into a place it can't see. Other obstacles include thick brush fences or drop fences with landings on a downhill slope. Courses always have water jumps, where horses jump over an obstacle into muddy waters. Horses can't see what's on the other side of most of these obstacles.

For that reason, riders first walk courses on foot so they can guide their horses safely over jumps. Riders pull on waterproof boots to slog through water obstacles. They count the number of strides between jumps to know when to slow a horse for a downhill jump or speed up for an uphill jump.

Horses trust their riders because those riders have gone before them and have seen every path and obstacle. We can't see into the future, but we can trust that God, our Navigator, has gone before us and has seen everything that's ahead.

The dark places you fear? They aren't dark to God; they're as bright as day. Uphill challenges? He'll give you strength and power to get over them. Bogged down in muddy problems? God knows the way through. Best of all, he'll never abandon you and will guide you over every obstacle.

CORRAL YOUR THOUGHTS: Are you facing an obstacle or problem? Write to God about it below.

GALLOP INTO ACTION: How has God helped you through challenges in the past? Write a prayer thanking him for his guidance.

FUN NOTES FROM THE BARN: Because eventing has three phases—dressage, cross-country jumping, and show jumping—it's called a triathlon.

42

GYMKHANA

Games on Horseback

A friend is always loyal.

PROVERBS 17:17

HAVE YOU EVER COMPETED in egg-and-spoon races at your school or a picnic? While walking as fast as you can between two points, you try to keep the egg on your spoon. Eggs roll and slide in unexpected ways and make a big splat when dropped. Now imagine doing this from the back of a horse. That's gymkhana!

People have probably been playing horseback games for as long as people have loved horses and riding. The Blackfoot Native American tribe played games on horseback called *omoksees*.[3] They'd gallop alongside a running buffalo to slap it or lean over to pick up something from the ground.

Today in the world of horse activities, events with many different games on horseback are called gymkhanas. Gymkhana competitions are popular all over the world, and children's groups like Pony Clubs and 4-H groups, as well as adult riding groups, often sponsor gymkhana events.

3. Historically, the Blackfoot tribe have called themselves the Niitsitapi.

The egg-and-spoon race is just one of many games played at gymkhana competitions. In polebending races, riders and their horses weave in and out around a line of vertical poles. Whoever completes the course the fastest while knocking over the fewest poles wins.

Musical mats, like musical chairs, has one less mat than the number of riders. Contestants ride around a circle of small mats on the ground. When the whistle blows, they leap off their horses to run and sit on a mat while still holding their horses. In stepping-stone competitions, overturned buckets are arranged in a line. Riders race their horses to the buckets, jump off, and step along the top of each bucket while holding onto their horses. At the end of the line, they hop back in the saddle and gallop back to the starting point.

Gymkhana events are competitive, but because they are often played in teams, they're also a fun way to make friends with others who share a love for horses. Riders enjoy friends and fun while learning riding skills and horse care. Having good friends is one of the blessings God has given us.

The event's leaders try to help riders learn how to be kind, whether they win or lose. This is also important in friendships. The ups and downs of friendships are a challenge, but Jesus, who is your very best friend, can help you learn to be a kind and loyal friend too.

CORRAL YOUR THOUGHTS: Gymkhana teammates are loyal to each other and work through difficult games together. Write about a time when you and a friend had to work through a difficulty.

GALLOP INTO ACTION: Thank a friend who has been loyal and plan a fun get-together to celebrate your friendship.

FUN NOTES FROM THE BARN: Pony Club began in England in 1929 as a fun way to teach riding skills and horse care to children. Pony Clubs now exist all over the world. 4-H clubs began in the US in 1902 as a way to encourage good agricultural practices. Today there are clubs all over the US, and many have horse care and riding programs.

43

DRIVING IN TEAMS

A Pair or More

Take my yoke upon you. Let me teach you, because I am humble and gentle at heart, and you will find rest for your souls.

MATTHEW 11:28-29

IT'S HARD TO IMAGINE TODAY, but until the early 1900s, horses moved just about everyone and everything. If a fire raged, teams of horses hauled the clanging fire engines to the scene. When doctors needed to make house calls to deliver a baby or stitch up a cut, they **hitched** up their horse and buggy. Horses pulled artillery guns in wars and harvesting machines on farms.

Gradually, motorized vehicles took over those jobs, and draft horses—horses that pulled vehicles—disappeared from most cities and rural areas. Work and carriage breeds like Shires and Friesians dwindled in numbers. But today, many groups work to preserve these breeds, and **driving** is popular again for recreation and competitions.

Whether drivers are enjoying a drive along a pleasant country road or whipping and zipping around cones in competitions, they must choose the number of horses needed for the weight of their cart and the conditions of their route. Single horses of many breeds are strong enough to pull a small cart with one or two people. But teams of various sizes are needed if the carriage is larger or the road is hilly, muddy, or snowy.

Teams of two or more horses can be hitched up together in different ways. A common arrangement for two-horse teams is side by side in what's called a **pair**. If the two horses are hitched one in front of the other, they're in **tandem**. A **unicorn arrangement** is when a third horse is hitched in front of a pair of horses. It can be exciting to watch four high-stepping horses hitched together in two pairs to pull a large carriage. The pair next to the carriage are called **wheelhorses**, and the pair in front are the **leaders**. Only experienced drivers can handle the reins of four horses at once, in what's called a four-in-hand.

Drivers watch for horses that are tired or overloaded, especially on rough roads. These horses can drag down the rest of the team. We also can get tired or overloaded by too much in our schedules or when hard things happen. But remember, when you feel weak, Jesus wants you to lean on him. When you're paired with him, he'll be the strong leader of your team, and he'll keep you from getting tired or dragged down, no matter how heavy the load or rough the road.

CORRAL YOUR THOUGHTS: Do you sometimes feel overwhelmed by schoolwork or extra activities? Write a prayer to God sharing with him how you feel and asking for his help.

GALLOP INTO ACTION: Pick a chore and ask a friend or sibling to team up with you to complete it. Then help them with one of their chores.

FUN NOTES FROM THE BARN: In a type of competition called combined driving, there are three phases. In the dressage phase, teams drive in different patterns and gaits. In the marathon phase, teams navigate obstacles over several miles. In the final phase, teams drive through a course of cones without knocking any over.

44

THERAPY HORSES

Gentle Helpers

Let your gentleness be evident to all.

PHILIPPIANS 4:5, NIV

THE MINIATURE HORSE STOOD QUIETLY, peering through his bushy black forelock at the young children clustered around him. The mini, who was part of a local therapeutic horse program, had come to the children's school to help teach them good communication skills. The children were learning how horses show their feelings through body language—how people and animals communicate with movements and expressions.

"When horses relax," the speaker said, "they point their ears up and forward. A horse being ridden often points one ear back to listen to its rider. But an angry or upset horse may pin its ears right back against its head. You children can't move your ears like horses," she went on, "but can you show us how you look when you're happy or angry or sad?" Hands shot up. All the children wanted to act out how they show feelings, even those who often stayed silent. After the lesson, everyone patted and hugged the mini that made learning so much fun.

Programs with specially trained therapy horses exist all over the world. Miniature horses and large draft horses—and every size in between—can make good therapy horses. Their gentleness helps children and adults find healing and hope for many physical and emotional challenges.

There are programs for riders who have physical disabilities and need special equipment or instruction. The motion of a horse's walk is similar to ours, so riding can improve a rider's muscle strength, balance, and flexibility, skills that are essential for walking. Riding also provides outdoor freedom and recreation. Unmounted activities like grooming a horse or reading to one can help children or adults with other physical or learning challenges.

Some speech therapists and mental health professionals use horses as part of their therapy too. When people in the military or first responders like police officers and firefighters have physical and emotional trauma from their jobs, therapy horses can help them heal.

Sometimes people don't know how to treat a person with a disability or someone who is struggling emotionally, but therapy horses seem to understand just what each person needs. As a follower of Jesus, you can ask the Holy Spirit to help you become more like Jesus by showing gentleness and compassion to those who are disabled or hurting.

CORRAL YOUR THOUGHTS: One way to show gentleness and understanding of another's needs is to be a good listener. Write down some topics you could use to start a conversation and make a new friend.

GALLOP INTO ACTION: Do you have a neighbor or classmate who may need you to show them compassion? Pray and ask Jesus to show you ways to be a friend to them.

FUN NOTES FROM THE BARN: Calm and friendly horses of all types, from miniature horses to huge Clydesdales, can make good therapy horses. Older horses often do well. Once they are chosen for a program, the horses are trained to walk calmly on a lead rope. Their handlers help desensitize them to equipment like wheelchairs and walkers and teach them to tolerate unexpected noises and movements on and around them.

45

TRAIL RIDING

Life Is an Adventure

"I know the plans I have for you," says the LORD. "They are plans for good and not for disaster, to give you a future and a hope."

JEREMIAH 29:11

IMAGINE IT'S A SUMMER DAY, and you and your friends are riding your horses along a forested path. You hear the creak of your saddle, and in the trees, birds twitter and squirrels chatter. The warm scent of pine trees surrounds you. Through the trees you catch glimpses of a blue lake. Trail rides—sometimes called hacks—are a fun way to relax with your horse and enjoy God's creation.

There are also competitions for trail riders, but these aren't races. On trail rides of ten to fifteen miles, horse and rider teams navigate obstacles along the trail. The obstacles can include opening and riding through gates, trotting over ground poles, or splashing across a stream. Judges on the trail look at the rider's horsemanship, and veterinarians check the horse's fitness. Riders earn points for their abilities and their horse's manners.

Some riders enjoy even bigger challenges. Endurance events of twenty-five to one hundred miles often go over mountains and other difficult terrains to really test a horse and rider's abilities and stamina. Vet checks before and after the event are required. Riders take regular rest stops on the trail to check their horse's pulse, breathing, soundness, and hydration. The goal is to finish with a horse that could still go on. In endurance competitions, one of the most desired awards is the BC—the Best Condition prize. This award is for the horse who finishes in the top ten for time and is also in the best condition of those top ten horses at the end of the race.

Trail riding is full of adventures, but you need basic skills and knowledge to be safe and successful. It's wise to ride along with someone who's done the type of trail riding you're interested in. They can help you set reasonable goals, answer your questions, and keep you on the right trail.

Life is full of adventures too. Sometimes, it's like a fun ride along a shady path. Other times, obstacles will test your abilities. Once in a while, life may seem like a long, hard endurance race. But you don't ride alone. God is on the trail with you. He has a plan for you and will help you set good goals and answer your questions. He'll keep you on the right path through all life's adventures.

CORRAL YOUR THOUGHTS: What kind of "trail ride" are you on right now? Use your journaling lines to describe it.

GALLOP INTO ACTION: Talk with your parents or another godly adult about their life adventures and how God was with them and helped them.

FUN NOTES FROM THE BARN: Some Western horse shows have trail classes in an arena, in which horse and rider teams must ride over and around things like noisy tarps, cross narrow bridges, and turn in small spaces.

46

PROTECTIVE GEAR

Staying Safe

Be strong in the Lord and in his mighty power. Put on all of God's armor so that you will be able to stand firm against all strategies of the devil.

EPHESIANS 6:10-11

• • • • • • • • • •

IN THE EARLY AMERICAN WEST, cowboys herding wild Texas longhorns up the Santa Fe trail or branding cattle on a Wyoming ranch needed protective gear. Their world was still wild and dangerous. Large hats shielded them from sun and rain, and boots and **chaps** (leather leg coverings) protected them from brush and cow horns.

While Western hats and chaps aren't necessary for most riders today, boots are still important for safety. The raised heels of English and Western boots keep the rider's feet from slipping through the stirrups. Boots also provide support and protection for the rider's ankles and calves.

Today most riders also wear a helmet that meets current safety standards and has been certified by the Safety Equipment Institute (SEI), an affiliate of ASTM International. Certified helmets have millions of gas bubbles arranged inside their layers. It's like wrapping your head in Bubble Wrap, and the bubbles work much the same way. If a rider hits their head, the bubbles begin to pop, slowing down the speed of the impact. That can make injuries less severe. The United States Equestrian Federation (USEF) now requires helmets at all nationally recognized eventing and dressage shows. No more top hats in dressage. Safety experts suggest that riders, especially children, wear helmets whenever they're around horses.

Another piece of protective gear is a vest. Layers of foam in riding vests protect a person's chest, abdomen, and internal organs. Eventing competitions require competitors in the cross-country phase to wear protective vests. Some people also wear them when working with young or difficult horses. Horseback riding is lots of fun, but a fall from a horse may cause injuries. So safety engineers have developed this equipment to keep riders safer.

There is much in this world that is enjoyable, but it can also be dangerous. The Bible says the devil seeks to spread pain and fear and violence everywhere. But you don't need to be afraid, because the Lord has given you protective armor against the devil.

So put on your helmet of salvation in Christ. Wear your shoes or boots that make you ready with his gospel of peace. And don't forget the breastplate or vest that protects you with the righteousness of Christ. The devil's evil plans can't harm you when you wear God's powerful protective gear.

CORRAL YOUR THOUGHTS: What are some things that make you anxious or even fearful?

GALLOP INTO ACTION: Read Ephesians 6:10-18 to discover all the protective gear that God has given you.

FUN NOTES FROM THE BARN: Riders may now choose helmets with an added layer of very strong plastic called a Multi-Directional Impact Protection System, or MIPS. It provides better protection against falls to the side.

47

GROOMING TIME

Looking Good

**Purify me from my sins,
and I will be clean;
wash me, and I will be
whiter than snow.**

PSALM 51:7

THOSE WHO LOVE HORSES take time to groom them so they look good and stay healthy. Grooming time is special—you're not asking the horse for anything, just caring for him. Grooming time is also a quiet time to talk and bond with your horse and check for any health issues like cuts, ticks, pain, or swelling. Most horses enjoy your undivided attention, and that deepens your relationship with a horse.

Keeping a horse clean and comfortable requires certain tools that both Western and English riders use. Most riders begin with a rubber currycomb that has nubby little bumps, moving it in circular motions to loosen dirt and hair. Next, comes a stiff bristle brush to whisk away that dirt and hair with short flicking movements. You shouldn't use either the currycomb or the stiff brush on sensitive areas like a horse's face or legs.

Following the stiff brush, many people use a soft bristle brush to remove fine dust and make the horse's coat glow. They also use that brush on the horse's face and legs. Manes and tails may be gently detangled using a brush with widely spaced, coated bristles, or even your hands. Riders must always clean out dirt and pebbles from the horse's hooves with a hoof pick.

Do you have a grooming routine for yourself? Washing and taking care of your hair and teeth will help you stay healthy and look your best. But the Bible says that being clean on the inside—in your heart—is even more important to God.

Having a daily routine of a quiet time with the Lord builds your relationship with him and helps keep your heart clean. When you read and think about his Word, it's like using a currycomb to bring up things you may need to ask his forgiveness for. When you tell him you're sorry, your heavenly Father forgives you and whisks your sins away. You can know that you have his undivided attention and can trust that he'll always be there to listen and forgive you.

CORRAL YOUR THOUGHTS: In the journaling section, write down one or two of your unkind words or actions from this week. For each one, write what would have been kinder to say or do.

GALLOP INTO ACTION: Stop and ask for God's forgiveness for any unkind words or actions. Ask him to wash you clean for Jesus' sake and to help you change.

FUN NOTES FROM THE BARN: Did you know that horses' manes and tails must meet certain length and style requirements for shows? Standards are different for each breed and kind of event, so some people make money at shows by helping riders prepare their horses.

48

HOOF CARE

A Firm Foundation

Trust in the LORD always, for the LORD GOD is the eternal Rock.

ISAIAH 26:4

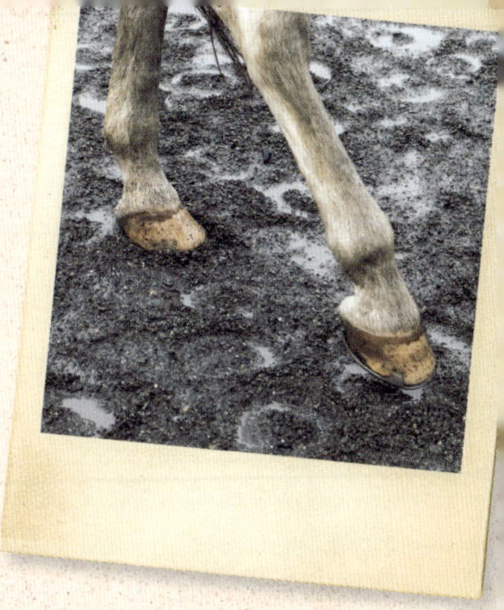

HOW OFTEN DO YOU need to get a haircut or trim your nails? A horse's hooves are made of the same protein—keratin—that gives structure to your nails and hair. And like hair and nails, hooves grow. It would take your fingernails close to a year to grow one inch beyond the end of your fingers. But in a year, a horse could grow a whole new hoof.

Wild horses keep on the move, often over rocky land, so their hooves usually wear down naturally. Domestic horses live mostly in stalls and pastures, with softer ground underfoot. They also don't get to move around as much as their wild cousins, so whether they wear shoes or not, horses need to have their hooves trimmed about every six to eight weeks. In the past, blacksmiths shoed horses in addition to working on things like wagons and plows. Today an equine specialist called a farrier cares for and shoes horses' hooves. Farriers work hard and need a good knowledge and understanding of horses.

During a farrier's visit, he or she trims and shapes a horse's hooves, replaces old shoes if necessary, and looks for signs of lameness or hoof disease. Not all horses need shoes, but many need them to be better balanced or to correct various problems. If a horse is ridden a lot on rocky ground, it may need shoes to keep its hooves from wearing down too quickly or to prevent chipping and cracking. Horses that work on snowy or icy ground may need special shoes to keep snow from packing into the hoof and may use **studs** to improve traction. Farriers help horse owners decide what's best for an individual horse.

For many horses, shoes help keep their hooves healthy and give them a firm foundation for whatever kind of work they do. Sometimes you may find yourself in situations where you feel like you're losing your footing. You might be tempted to chase fads that shift like sand every few months. You might get mired in muddy arguments with siblings or slip into anger over family rules that seem unfair.

The Bible promises that Jesus is a solid rock that you can build your life on. When you trust in him and follow his teachings, you will always be on a firm foundation.

CORRAL YOUR THOUGHTS: Write down some ways you can build your life on the solid foundation of Jesus Christ so that you can keep your footing in tough situations.

GALLOP INTO ACTION: Write out Isaiah 26:4 in the middle of a large piece of paper. Then draw horses that are keeping their footing on tough terrain all around the verse. Display your drawing to remind yourself to trust God and stand firm.

FUN NOTES FROM THE BARN: It may look scary when a farrier pounds nails into a horse's hooves, but the nails go painlessly through a part of the hoof similar to the part of your fingernail you cut.

49

BRIDLES

Hold Me, Guide Me

If I rise on the wings of the dawn, if I settle on the far side of the sea, even there your hand will guide me, your right hand will hold me fast.

PSALM 139:9-10, NIV

WHICH INVENTION DO YOU think came first? The bridle or the saddle? Ancient art from China, Egypt, and Rome shows that horses wore bridles long before saddles. In those artworks, the bridles look a lot like today's bridles. Some were simple ones of leather or rope. Gold and silver glittered on others. A few were adorned with ribbons and tassels. Today most bridles fall into two categories, depending on the type of riding you do—English or Western.

A basic English bridle goes up around the horse's ears and down each side of its head. Other straps wrap around the nose, brow, and throat to keep the bridle from slipping off. The reins attach to rings on the bit. On a bitless bridle, the reins attach to rings on the noseband.

Western bridles are similar to English bridles. But they may loop up around just one ear, and they may not have additional bands. Like English bridles, reins attach to rings on the bit, or on the noseband if there's no bit. One type of bitless Western bridle has a rounded rawhide noseband called a **bosal**. The reins attach to the bosal under the horse's chin.

Whether you use an English or Western bridle, it works together with the reins for the same purpose—to guide the horse on the right path and hold it to the right speed. In arenas, riders guide their horses in circles or over jumps. On trails, wise riders hold their horses to a walk when splashing across rocky streams.

Do you ever wonder what paths you'll take when you grow up? Perhaps you'd like to teach math or play in a band. Or do you want to write adventure stories? You may sometimes feel a little anxious about choosing the path that's right for you, but the Lord promises to guide you as you grow. He'll help you discover more about your interests and talents. Even if you have to splash through a few rocky streams or jump some tall fences, your loving heavenly Father holds your hand and guides you.

CORRAL YOUR THOUGHTS: Write down one or two concerns you have about your future. Next to each concern, write about how you can trust God with it.

GALLOP INTO ACTION: Think of a career you're interested in and the skills you might need for it. Ask God to guide you to opportunities to learn and practice those skills with your family, at school, or in your church or community. You may find new interests and skills for the future *and* help others at the same time.

FUN NOTES FROM THE BARN: English show bridles have few decorations, but Western show bridles often have embellishments such as silver, beading, or designs stamped or carved into the leather.

50

FLY MASKS

Guard Your Heart

Guard your heart above all else, for it determines the course of your life.

PROVERBS 4:23

DO YOU ENJOY SUMMER, when you can ride your bike or splash in the pool? What you probably don't enjoy, though, are biting bugs and painful sunburns. Horses love to be outside in the summer, too, but they're bothered by those same bugs. They can even get sunburns, especially on their noses. While you can slather on sunscreen, wear long sleeves, and use bug spray to prevent burns and keep those pesky insects away, horses need different solutions.

When it's hot and buggy, people may turn their horses out to pasture covered in screens from head to hoof. Not the kind you have in your windows, of course—but soft, flexible screens that fit the parts of a horse. These are called fly masks, fly sheets, and fly boots. Not all horses need full body protection. Some horses are more sensitive, and some pastures have more insects. But lots of horses wear fly masks, because bugs love the fluids around a horse's eyes and nostrils and the tender skin inside its ears.

Fly masks come in many styles and sizes for different breeds and for the needs of each horse. Some have ear covers and an opening for the horse's forelock. For horses that are especially sensitive to the sun, there are fly masks that cover more of the nose or have a built-in sun visor. Many masks are chemically treated to provide protection against sunburn and eye damage. For horses that spend the night outside, fly masks can come with reflective strips. Masks can keep out dust and protect healing wounds, and they need to fit snugly but allow the ears to move. Because horses like to roll and scratch, fly masks must also be sturdy.

Horses like to relax out in a pasture, but itchy mosquito bites and clouds of tiny gnats can stress horses out and cause disease. Fly masks protect their sensitive eyes and ears from harm.

In a similar way, you may like to relax by reading books or listening to music or watching movies and television. Lots of these provide good entertainment, but some have inappropriate pictures or information that could hurt you and lead your heart away from your heavenly Father. Just as a fly mask guards a horse's eyes and ears, you can protect your heart by guarding your eyes and ears.

CORRAL YOUR THOUGHTS: On your journaling lines, list some of the books, music, movies, and television shows you've relaxed with recently. Draw a heart next to the ones that had a message of kindness, love, goodness, or truth.

GALLOP INTO ACTION: Fly masks screen out bad bugs. Talk with your parents about ways you can screen out the wrong kinds of entertainment and protect your heart.

FUN NOTES FROM THE BARN: Some horse owners cover their horses in zebra-striped fly masks and sheets. A few studies have shown that the irregular zebra pattern confuses bugs and discourages them from landing.

51

SADDLES

Which One Is Best?

If you need wisdom, ask our generous God, and he will give it to you.

JAMES 1:5

WHEN YOU LOOK AT SADDLES, you may wonder how riders choose one from the many styles and sizes available. But most saddles, even English and Western ones, have a lot in common. Almost all saddles have a wooden or synthetic foundation, called a **tree**, that establishes the saddle's size and determines how it sits on the horse. All saddles have a backrest called a **cantle** and a rounded **pommel** on the front. Every saddle must have straps to hold the saddle on the horse. On both Western and English saddles, stirrups hang from narrow or wide straps.

Of course, there are differences between Western and English saddles. The biggest difference is probably that Western saddles have a **horn** and English saddles don't. English saddles are also smaller and lighter. Within these two categories, riders choose styles that work best for their horse activity. For example, an English jumping saddle has a flat seat and short, rounded saddle flaps so riders can more easily rise out of the seat for jumps. Dressage riders need a saddle with a deep seat to help them sit straight and tall even through a bumpy trot.

Western riders have choices too. Ranch workers need a comfortable saddle for all-day work and a strong horn to hold a roped cow that's struggling to get away. Barrel racers often choose a Western saddle with a deeper seat and a tall horn to hold when their horse leans into a tight turn around a barrel. No saddle is wrong, but it's important to choose the saddle that's best for you and the type of riding you do. If you choose an English jumping saddle to do barrel racing, you could be hurt.

In the world, you have choices too. Do you want to join the school's art club or start playing in the school band? What movie will you and your friends choose to watch? Someday you'll have choices about what you want to do as an adult. How will you choose what's best for you? Your heavenly Father promises to give you wisdom to make good choices, and because he created your innermost being, he knows which choices will be exactly the right ones for you.

CORRAL YOUR THOUGHTS: Are you struggling to make a choice about something? Make a list of the pros and cons for each option.

GALLOP INTO ACTION: Riders ask an expert for help in choosing the right saddle. Pray and then talk with your expert—a parent or trusted adult—about your choices.

FUN NOTES FROM THE BARN: The same saddle parts have different names in English and Western riding. English riders call the strap that holds a saddle on a **girth**. Western riders call it a **cinch**. On English saddles, the narrow straps that hang down to hold the stirrups are called **stirrup leathers**; on Western saddles, these are usually wider and are called **fenders**.

52

STIRRUPS

Better Support

Give your burdens to the LORD, and he will take care of you. He will not permit the godly to slip and fall.

PSALM 55:22

• • • • • • • • •

"WARM-UP IS OVER," called the instructor. "Cross your stirrups over the front of your saddle, and let's work on your balance." Riders may groan, but riding without stirrups does improve a rider's balance. On the other hand, it takes away the extra support that stirrups provide, which helps steady riders through a bumpy trot or a long trail ride.

Long ago, everyone rode without stirrups because they weren't invented until long after people began riding horses. Archaeologists have found the earliest evidence of the use of stirrups in Asia, dating between AD 200 and 300, so historians think stirrups may have been invented there. Stirrups then spread to the nomadic tribes of Central Asia. Supported by their stirrups, these warriors rode rings around other horsemen and shot arrows with more power and accuracy. Nomadic tribes moved farther and farther west, taking the technology of stirrups with them.

By the sixth century AD, Byzantine military manuals showed the use of stirrups. But other Western armies still rode without stirrups, and they lost battles to the Eastern warriors, who rode with better support. Europeans soon learned the value of stirrups, and by medieval times, stirrups made knights on horseback almost unbeatable. With stirrups, the knights could ride with greater boldness, and it was harder to unseat them in close combat.

Modern stirrups still have the same basic shape as ancient stirrups, but they are now made of stainless steel, wood, or a combination of these. The sides of an English stirrup curve up from a flat base to form an opening for the foot. Above that is a small slit for the stirrup leather to go through. Some English stirrups have a breakaway feature so a rider's foot can't get caught if they fall. Western stirrups have a wooden or metal piece that curves down and around the foot. At the top, a short bar attaches to the fender that hangs down on Western saddles. Sometimes Western stirrups are closed at the front to prevent a rider's foot from slipping through.

Before stirrups, riders could fall when riding fast or in battle. In life, hard situations at school, with friends, and in our families can come at us fast.

Some situations are short bumps, while others are longer. Either way, you may feel like you're falling, but God will never let you fall. Stirrups support riders through jolting trots and long trail rides. Your heavenly Father promises to support you through every bump or long, hard situation.

CORRAL YOUR THOUGHTS: How has God supported you in bumpy times? Write about it below.

GALLOP INTO ACTION: If you know someone who needs support, pray for them and then write a note to strengthen and encourage them.

FUN NOTES FROM THE BARN: Western saddles usually come with stirrups, but you often have to buy the stirrups separately for English saddles.

Glossary of Horse Terms

Akhal-Teke—an ancient breed with a metallic golden coat and a slender form that originated in Turkmenistan

American Curly horse (or Bashkir Curly horse)—a horse breed found in North America that has an unusual curly coat

Appaloosa—a hardy and sure-footed breed of horses with beautiful spotted coats, originally bred by the Nez Percé people

Arabian—an ancient breed developed by Bedouin tribesmen, known for their elegant heads and great endurance

Arena—a large enclosed area in which horses can be ridden and trained and where horse competitions can take place

Bald face—white markings that cover a horse's entire face

Bars—a gap in a horse's mouth between the incisors and the molars

Bay—horses of various shades of brown coats with black points on the ears, mane, legs, and tail

Bearing rein—a type of rein used to pull carriage horses' heads high for a more elegant look, can sometimes be pulled too tight

Bit—a small bar made of different types of metal or synthetic materials, attached to a bridle and placed in a horse's mouth so the rider can guide it

Blaze—a white stripe on a horse's face

Bosal—a rounded rawhide noseband found on a specific type of Western bridle

Brand—to use a hot iron or freeze branding to mark livestock to show ownership; also the name of the hot iron used for branding

Bridle—leather headgear for horses that functions with the bit and reins to guide the horse

Buckskin—a horse with a light, dark, or reddish deer hide color; some have dark brown or black manes, legs, and tails

Canter—a fast gait, quicker than a trot but slower than a gallop

Canter pirouette—a dressage skill in which the horse makes a full circle around a stationary back hoof

Cantle—the backrest of a saddle

Capriole—a dressage leap in which the horse kicks out with its hind legs

Caspian horse—a gentle and elegant pony-size horse originating in the mountains of Northern Iran

Cavalry—a unit of horses and riders used as part of an army

Cecum—a digestive organ that, in horses, helps process large amounts of fibrous food

Chaps—leather leggings worn most often by Western riders for protection in rough country or as part of a traditional Western costume in shows

Chestnut—horses with various shades of reddish coats and reddish or light-colored manes and tails

Cinch—the strap used to hold a Western saddle on a horse

Cloverleaf pattern—a pattern run by barrel

racers that is in the shape of a three-leaf clover

Clydesdale—a sturdy breed of draft horses known for their white feathered legs; originating in Scotland

Color breed—a registry of horses based on their coat color rather than their breed or breed type

Colt—a young male horse up to the age of three

Coronet—a thin white marking just above a horse's hoof, shorter than a sock or stocking

Cross-country jumping—one of the three phases of an eventing triathlon, involving jumping challenging solid obstacles

Curb bit—a type of bit that puts pressure on a horse's mouth, chin, and on the top of its head using shanks on each side of the bit and a curb chain or strap

Dartmoor pony—a hardy English breed often used as mounts for children

Dished profile—a profile that curves inward, characteristic of Arabian horses

Draft horse—large, powerful horses, such as Shires and Clydesdales, typically used for farmwork or hauling wagons

Dressage—a horse-training system developed long ago to make horses more balanced and supple; now a popular and competitive riding activity

Drill team—a Western event in which a team of riders guides their horses in synchronized movements choreographed to music

Driving—guiding a horse or team of horses to pull a carriage or cart

Eventing—a triathlon competition involving three phases: dressage, cross-country jumping, and show jumping

Farrier—a horse specialist who cares for and shoes horses' hooves

Feathers (or Feathering)—long, thick hair that grows down from the lower part of some horses' legs

Fenders—wide leather straps that hold the stirrups on a Western saddle

Feral horse—a horse born and living in the wild but descended from domesticated horses that escaped

Filly—a young female horse up to three years old

Float—to file down the sharp points on a horse's teeth so they wear more evenly

Foal—a young horse of either sex, under a year old

Forelock—the part of a horse's or pony's mane that falls between its ears onto its face

Friesian—a large, noble-looking horse known for its grace and black coat; originating in Friesland, a province of the Netherlands

Frog—a triangular structure on the bottom of a horse's hoof that cushions the force of the horse's steps

Gait—one of various ways a horse can move; the four basic gaits are the walk, trot, canter, and gallop

Gaited horse—a horse with more than the four basic gaits

Gallop—the fastest of the four basic gaits

Girth—the strap used to hold an English saddle on a horse

Groom—a person whose job is to care for horses

Ground poles—poles that are placed on the ground and spaced various distances apart for training horses

Gymkhana—an event in which riders and their horses compete in team games

Gypsy Vanner horse—a breed developed by the

Roma people after World War II, that have long, flowing manes and tails and may have pinto markings

Hack—a trail ride

Hand—a unit roughly the width of an adult's hand, or four inches, used to measure a horse's height; the expression "hands high" is abbreviated "hh"

Herd—a group of horses

Hitch—to harness one or more horses to a vehicle so they can pull it

Hock—a joint on a horse's hind leg similar in function to the human ankle

Horn—a prominent knob on the pommel of a Western saddle, often used to anchor a lasso

Icelandic horse—an extremely pure gaited horse bred in Iceland

Interdental space—a wide gap between a horse's incisors and molars

Jockey—a person who rides horses professionally in races

Leaders—in carriage driving, the front pair of horses

Lipizzan (or Lipizzaner)—Spanish-bred horses with high-set tails, large eyes, short legs, and muscular bodies; most famous for their beautiful dressage dances at the Spanish Riding School in Austria

Mare—an adult female horse

Morgan—a small but strong American breed developed by Justin Morgan

Mustang—intelligent and hardy horses whose ancestors escaped from Spanish explorers and now live in feral herds throughout the western United States

Muzzle—a horse's jaw and nose

Nicker—a gentle, low sound a horse makes as a greeting or call

Noseband—the part of a halter or bridle that wraps around a horse's nose

Overo—a paint or pinto coat pattern, typically describing a dark horse with jagged white patches that rarely go across the back, dark legs, a white face, and a single-color tail

Pace—a fast gait of some horses where the legs on the same side move together

Packhorse—a horse used to carry goods, such as equipment or camping supplies

Paint—a breed of horses with at least one parent registered with the American Paint Horse Registry; the other parent may be a Quarter Horse, Thoroughbred, or another Paint

Pair—a two-horse team hitched side by side

Palomino—a horse with a golden coat and a light mane and tail

Paso Fino—a breed of gaited horses whose earliest ancestry was Spanish, but who have been further developed in South America and the Caribbean

Piaffe—the dressage skill of trotting in place

Pinto—a color breed with a spotted coat pattern

Pommel—the front of an English or Western saddle that rounds upward, giving some support

Post—when a rider rises up and down in the saddle to make a trot more comfortable

Prey animal—animals who must stay on guard against other animals who may wish to eat them

Purebred—a horse whose parents and ancestors are from the same breed

Quadrille—a group of four or more horse-and-rider pairs performing patterns to music

Quarter Horse—an American breed known for their muscular hindquarters, fast sprints, and "cow sense"; one of the most popular horse breeds

Reciprocal apparatus—a group of tendons and

muscles that work together to stabilize the upper joints of the hind legs to keep a horse's legs from folding while it sleeps standing up

Reins—straps that connect to a horse's bit and are used to direct the horse

Running walk—a smooth but fast gait that some gaited horses have

Saddle—a padded seat, typically leather, used for a rider's comfort and security on horseback

Shetland pony—one of the smallest pony breeds, native to the Shetland Islands off the north coast of Scotland

Shire—a tall British draft horse with feathered legs; usually black, bay, or gray

Shoe—a U-shaped piece of metal nailed to a horse's hoof to protect it from wear; also the action of nailing a shoe to a horse's hoof

Show jumping—a competitive event where a horse and rider must jump obstacles in an arena, often within a time limit

Snaffle bit—a type of bit that puts direct pressure on the tongue and the sides and corners of a horse's mouth

Snip—a white marking on a horse's nose

Sock—a white leg marking that begins at the

hoof and ends below the knee or hock; wider than a coronet but shorter than a stocking

Stallion—an adult male horse able to father offspring

Standardbred—an American breed descended from Thoroughbred and Morgan lines, often used for harness racing

Star—a white marking between a horse's eyes

Stay apparatus—a grouping of muscles, tendons, and ligaments on the front legs and the lower hind legs that help ensure that a horse's legs stay stable while it sleeps standing up

Stifle—a joint on a horse's hind leg similar in function to the human knee

Stirrup leathers—narrow leather straps that hold the stirrups on an English saddle

Stirrups—wood or metal U-shaped rings that hang from a saddle and support the rider's foot

Stocking—a white leg marking that extends from the hoof to above the knee or hock

Stride—the length of a horse's step

Studs—projections on a special horseshoe intended to provide better traction, similar to cleats on sports shoes

Tack—the equipment, such as halters, saddles, bridles, and bits, used to work with horses

Tandem—an arrangement of horses in which one is hitched in front of the other

Tennessee Walking horse (or Tennessee Walker)—an American breed of gaited horses often used for trail riding

Thoroughbred—a breed of horses originating in England in the seventeenth century, often used for racing but also in sports such as jumping, dressage, and eventing

Tobiano—a pinto coat pattern characterized by round or oval white markings, with white legs and often a two-colored tail; the coat may be mostly dark-colored or mostly white

Tolt—a high-stepping running walk possessed by Icelandic horses

Tovero—a rare paint or pinto coat pattern that combines features of the tobiano and overo patterns to create a mostly white horse with color on the ears and head; also called medicine hat or war bonnet horses

Tree—the wooden or synthetic foundation of a saddle

Trot—a medium gait, faster than a walk but slower than a canter

Unicorn arrangement—an arrangement of horses in which a single horse is hitched in front of a side-by-side pair

Walk—the slowest of the horse's four basic gaits

Wean—when a young horse stops drinking its mother's milk and begins to eat regular foods

Wheelhorses—in carriage driving, the pair of horses closest to the carriage

Whinny—a loud sound a horse makes, often used to communicate and connect with other horses

Withers—the ridge between a horse's shoulder blades, which is the highest point of the back; horses are measured from the ground to this point

Wrangler—a person who handles and cares for horses

Learn More

IF YOU'D LIKE TO continue learning about horses, check out some of these books and websites. Be sure to ask a parent or caretaker for permission before going online. And if you read or see anything on a website or in a book that is different from what you believe about God, talk to a trusted adult.

Books

Clutton-Brock, Juliet. *Horse*. DK Eyewitness Books, 2008.

Hill, Cherry. *Cherry Hill's Horse Care for Kids: Grooming, Feeding, Behavior, Stable & Pasture, Health Care, Handling & Safety, Enjoying*. Storey Publishing, 2002.

Reeve, Moira C., and Sharon Biggs. *The Original Horse Bible: The Definitive Source for All Things Horse*. 2nd ed., CompanionHouse Books, 2021.

Websites

4-H Organization: 4-h.org

Breeds of Horses: breeds.okstate.edu/horses; this Oklahoma State University website also has links to many horse breed associations.

Professional Association of Therapeutic Horsemanship International (PATH Intl.): pathintl.org

United States Pony Club: ponyclub.org

United Kingdom Pony Club: pcuk.org

United States Equestrian Federation: usef.org; USEF is the national governing body for equestrian sports and has information and numerous videos about English and Western riding activities.

Acknowledgments

WHEN A HORSE AND RIDER enter a show or trail-riding competition, we may not realize the team it took to get them ready. Family and trainers, veterinarians and groomers—all had an important part in preparing that rider and horse to be the very best they could be. It's the same for a book, and I'm thankful to all those who helped *Hoofprints of Hope Devotional: 52 Wonders of Faith and Science for Horse-Loving Kids* gallop into the world.

My biggest thanks goes to my husband and best friend, Wes. Thank you for your love and making me laugh when I was discouraged, and for never letting me run out of chocolate! To my family and friends—I couldn't have written *Hoofprints* without your prayers and interest in the book's progress.

A special thanks to my agent, Dan Balow, who believed in *Hoofprints* and is a wonderful source of wisdom and knowledge about the publishing world. You've made the journey understandable and kept me on the correct trail.

The team at Tyndale has been fantastic. Linda Howard and Talia Messina, you embraced my vision for *Hoofprints* and enthusiastically shepherded it all along the trail. Debbie King, you were a gracious and patient editor, and I enjoyed working with you and your team, Claire Lloyd, Alyssa Durst, and Erin Gwynne, to get *Hoofprints* ready for horse lovers. I was thrilled to see the creativity of art director Jackie Nuñez and designer Eva Winters. You polished *Hoofprints* to a show-worthy shine with beautiful illustrations and designs.

Thank you, Andrea Martin and Wendie Connors, for making me feel a part of the Tyndale family and arranging a tour of Tyndale. Everyone was friendly and took time to talk. Thank you to Annette Taroli, Emily VanderBent, Megan D'Agostino, and the entire Tyndale team, for your kindness and help through the whole process.

A heartfelt thanks to my critique group, Denice, Janice, Kathryn, Lavonne, and Sue. You gave your time and expertise to help groom many *Hoofprint* devotions and stayed smiling and interested, no matter how many horse facts I tossed at you!

To my riding friends at Stable Strides, Meg, Debbie, and Nakita, Wharton and Phil, thanks for your encouragement when I began riding again after having to stop for several years. Kathryn and Alexa, thank you for sharing my excitement about *Hoofprints* and checking facts. Of course I can't forget Teddy, a friendly chestnut Tennessee Walker, who has become a kind equine partner.

Above all, thank you, Lord, for saving me and guiding me with your love along my trail each day. You created these amazing creatures called horses and made a way for me to love and enjoy them, and from those experiences write *Hoofprints* to encourage others to want to gallop through life with you.

DRESSAGE
SARATOGA

About the Author

KATHY O'NEILL was a horse-crazy kid who grew up in small-town Maine. Every week she rode her bike to the library to borrow horse books. On her great grandparents' farm, she listened to stories of when they kept farm horses. Later, on a farm tucked into the Maine woods, Kathy and her husband raised two children alongside goats and puppies and a pinto pony named Champ. Today Kathy lives in Colorado, where she is a teacher, writer, and speaker. She graduated from the University of Maine with an education degree and concentrations in art and child psychology. Following her husband's graduation from seminary, they've served in churches around the country. Kathy has taught in Christian schools, Sunday school, and homeschool groups. She's served on education committees and helped her husband in his ministry. And always the Lord has provided places for a still-horse-crazy girl to ride and enjoy horses. Visit her online at kathy-oneill.com.

KATHY-ONEILL.COM

Image Credits

Unless otherwise noted, cover and interior photographs are from Adobe Stock and are the property of their respective copyright holders, and all rights are reserved. Listed by page number:

i geometric pattern © Kate K.
i paper texture © Ian Barnard/Creative Market
iv hoofprints © Yana Lyso/Shutterstock
x pebble texture © dartlab
x two horses © Rita Kochmarjova
xi, 5 western icons © Yanka
xiv horses running © kwadrat70
2 fence icon © Puspa Kusuma/Thenounproject
2 gallop icon public domain by Pablo Barros da Silveira
2 cowboy hat icon © Muhammad Nur Auliady Pamungkas/Thenounproject
4 horse monoline © Wieslaw
5 signpost © Wieslaw
6 appaloosa © slowmotiongli
7 stars © Yanka
9 lasso © Yusif
10 Arabian horse © Olga Itina
11 Bay Arabian horse © rima15
11 old photo frame © U.P.images
14 Caspian horse © Mauritius71
18, 19 American Curly horses © Olena
22 Gypsy Vanner horse © Terri Cage
26 Icelandic horse © kathomenden
30 Lipizzaner horses in Vienna © Edyta BB
34 mustang © catahula
38 red pinto and foal © callipso88
39 American Paint horse © Rita Kochmarjova
42, 43 Quarter horses © lenkadan
46 miniature Shetland © Rita Kochmarjova
47 Shetland pony © Snapvision
50 Shire horses © Jenny Thompson
51 Aragon horse © Scully Pictures
54 equestrian dressage monoline © sahs94
56 Morgan horse, public domain
60 American Pony Express, public domain
64 black beauty illustration © Basicmoments
68, 81 Wyoming cowgirl © Terri Cage
72 Seabiscuit, public domain
76 Sergeant Reckless from U.S. Marine Corps Archives
80 Trigger, public domain
84 gray horse resting © яна винникова
85 gray horse looking away © ccestep8
88 Chincoteague © Bonnie U. Gruenberg/Wikimedia Commons
92 horse in winter © Maria Ivanushkina/500px

96 Snowman © VentnorNJ/Wikimedia Commons
97 horse jumping © Oleksandr Zastrozhnov
100 Mister Ed, public domain
101 Mister Ed cast, public domain
104 Molly the Pony © Jean Ogden Just Chaos Photography
108 Dartmoor pony foal © hardyuno
109 teddy bear in stall © katherine_gee
112, 162 monoline galloping horse legs © Wieslaw
114 horses embracing © byrdyak
118 horse head shot © Nigel Baker
119 chestnut gelding © mari
122 wild family © Fabrizio Sana
123 horse's ear © alzay
126 foal with mother © virgonira
127 mother and baby © Kimberley
130 chewing horse © marigo
131 horse teeth close-up © Nathan Allred
134 horse fed apple © RD-Fotografie
135 young funny horse © madredus
138 black horse runs © Julia Siomuha
139 sorrel horse © lenkadan
142 bay horse © Viktoria Makarova
146 sleeping horse © Unique Stock Art
147 horse sleeping in stable © Hanna Alandi
150 wild horses in dust © Mari_art
151 white horse running © Helena Lopes/Unsplash
154 clydesdale mare and foal © Gannet77/iStockphoto
155 clydesdale grazing © MEFlynn/iStockphoto
158 brown horse running © Philippe Oursel/Unsplash
159 hoof underneath © Ella
162 equestrian rider monoline © sahs94
164, 165 horses barrel racing © beatrix kido
168 running poles © Brandy Taylor/iStockphoto
172 horse jumping © muro
176 young cowgirl competing © Instants/iStockphoto
177 pole bending © btimages/iStockphoto
180 work horses reseting © Lisa Shoemaker/iStockphoto
184 horse with long mane © September
188 family horseback riding © Cathleen
189 riding in spring forest © vprotastchik
192 cowboy with chaps © ukterryg
196 dirty horse © chelle129
197 brushing horse © Chris Bair/Unsplash
200 filing hoof © Lena Bauermeister/Unsplash
201 close-up of horse legs © Greg Rosenke/Unsplash
204 braided horse with bridle © Tara
205 white horse in fenced area © Ümit Güneś/Unsplash
208 horse blindfold © Sinuswelle
212 cowboy western saddle © T L Peterson
213 English saddle © verdateo
216 stirrup © Alexia Khruscheva
220 horse herd running © kwadrat70
234 neighing horse close-up © MZaitsev

Front cover horses running © kwadrat70
Back cover Aragon horse © Scully Pictures